Wishing you great success!

Mike Parkinson's

Do-It-Yourself
Billion Dollar
Graphics

3 Fast and Easy Steps to Turn Your Text and Ideas Into Persuasive Graphics

PepperLip Press

Other fine tools and seminars are available. Visit **www.BillionDollarGraphics.com** to learn more.

All artwork, except where noted, was created by Mike Parkinson and 24 Hour Company. All graphics are devoid of proprietary content and, where applicable, permissions were granted to share the visuals with the general public. The following graphics were used with permission:

- page 65 - James Whistler's *Arrangement in Gray and Black: Portrait of the Artist's Mother.* Musee d'Orsay; Georges-Pierre Seurat's *A Sunday Afternoon on the Island of La Grand Jatte.* The Art Institution of Chicago; Edgar Degas' *Dancers Practicing at the Bar.* Metropolitan Museum of Art.
- pages 65 and 98 - shuttle graphic developed by NASA (nasa.gov)
- pages 74 and 97 - Bonneville Generator graphic developed by U.S. Amy Corps of Engineers (images.usace.army.mil)
- page 82 - revised New York City subway map developed by Kick Design (kickdesign.com)
- page 98 - shuttle wing graphic developed by NASA (nasa.gov)
- page 98 - compressor graphic developed by Bob Ulrich of Ulrich Digital (lrich@robertulrich.com)
- page 101 - flashlight graphic developed by Bob Ulrich of Ulrich Digital (lrich@robertulrich.com); engine diagram developed by Todd Harrison
- page 107 - aqualis (upper right) developed by Bob Ulrich of Ulrich Digital (lrich@robertulrich.com)
- page 114 - security X-ray compliments of U.S. Transportation Security Administration (tsa.gov)
- page 114 - Border Patrol Communication Center compliments of U.S. Army (army.mil)

Edited by Jennifer Parkinson, Nanna Ingvarsson, and Colleen Jolly.
Cover design by Mike Parkinson and interior design by Jennifer Parkinson and Mike Parkinson.
Printed by Signature Book Printing, www.sbpbooks.com
ISBN: 978-1-4507-4011-1

ABOUT THE AUTHOR

Mike Parkinson has spearheaded multi-billion dollar projects and created thousands of graphics resulting in billions of dollars in increased revenue for his clients. He is a multi-published author and is often requested to speak at national conferences, large and small companies, and graphic industry events.

Mike started his formal design training at the Baltimore School for the Arts. After four years of fine arts education, he attended the University of Maryland Baltimore County's Digital Arts Program. Upon graduation, he was hired as a graphic designer at a medical training company, where he was promoted to art director. Using his knowledge and understanding of visual communication, Mike has supported trial attorneys and created ad campaigns, tutorials, corporate briefings, Web portals, medical training software, and more. He was invited to become part owner of 24 Hour Company in 1999. Mike leveraged his design experience to help his partners transform the company into the industry leader. With over 20 years of experience, Mike shares the secrets of effective graphics with other professionals to help them realize their goals and dreams by increasing their success rates through better visual communication. In 2006, he founded Billion Dollar Graphics (www.BillionDollarGraphics.com) to offer articles, books, tools, and resources that provide secrets, tips, tricks, strategies, and best practices to non-designers and designers alike. In 2009, Mike launched BizGraphics On Demand (www.BizGraphicsOnDemand.com). BizGraphics On Demand is a growing library of low-cost, high-quality business and information graphics editable in PowerPoint. His goal is to empower everyone to use clear, compelling graphics to reach new heights of success.

DEDICATION

This book is dedicated to my wife, Jennifer.

ACKNOWLEDGEMENTS

Thank you to—in no particular order—Kathy Parkinson, Michael D. Parkinson, Barbara Parkinson, Betty Bock, Jeff Hall, Dennis Fitzgerald, Sandi Fitzgerald, Paul Kay, Von, Kay, Colleen Jolly, Robert Frey, Sheila McCarthy, Bob Ulrich, Connie Williams, Deanna Boudreau, Jay Schiavo, Denise Rhea-McKenzie, Debbie Rivera, Luis Figuera, Chris Prochaska, Marc Bolea, Nanna Ingvarsson, Kafi Johnson, Kevin Bush, Stacy Ross, Alvin Lowe, Kristi Arthur, Pat Bartlett, Lakin Jones, Debi Ratcliffe, Sheree Smith, Bridget Skelly, Jeanine Staab, Dana Thompson, Erycka Snyder, Derrick Pedranti, Chris Mahon, Kevin Beaumont, Steve Cummings, Megan Skuller, Joe Tedesco, Steve Kantor, Mo Fathelbab, Randy Morgan, Miles Fawcet, Griff Thomas, Beth Wingate, Ann Oliveri, Jack Banks, Mark Murphy, Stacia Kelly, M.J. Efflandt, Tony Arellano, Adam Ugolnik, and Pam Overton, David Winton, Andy Bounds, Rob Ransone, Chuck Keller, Bill Andre, Charlie Divine, Joe Jablonski, Barbara Esmedina, Chris Simmons, Jeanne Schulze, Kym Harrington, Elizabeth Goonan, Bobbie O'Brien, Ann Moss, Julia Maurer, Larry Tracy, Wendy Frieman, Carl Dickson, Diane Dickson, BJ Lownie, Azra Lownie, Jon Williams, and Olessia Smotrova-Taylor for your help and support.

Thanks to C2 Media (www.c2media.com), ENEXDI (www.enexdi.com), CapturePlanning.com, ProposalCafe.com, SalesEdge (www.salesedgellc.com), StrategicProposals (www.strategicproposals.com), PresentationXpert.com, Presenters and Programs Forum, Training Media Review (www.tmreview.com), Manage Smarter (www.managesmarter.com), Google (www.google.com), and the Association of Proposal Management Professionals (www.apmp.org).

A **very** special thank you to:

www.24hrco.com

To **everyone** who has helped and continues to help me with advice, ideas, and support, I extend a heartfelt thank you.

TABLE OF CONTENTS

Introduction: The Power of Graphics

What we see has a profound effect on what we do, how we feel, and who we are. Through experience and experimentation, we continually increase our understanding of the visual world and how we are influenced by it. Psychologist Albert Mehrabian demonstrated that 93% of communication is nonverbal.* Research at 3M Corporation concluded that **we process visuals 60,000 times faster than text.** Other studies found that the human brain deciphers image elements simultaneously, while language is decoded in a linear, sequential manner taking more time to process.

Relatively speaking, in terms of communication, textual ubiquity is brand new. Thanks to millions of years of evolution, we are genetically wired to respond differently to visuals than text. For example, humans have an innate fondness for images of wide, open landscapes, which evoke an instant sense of well-being and contentment. Psychologists hypothesize that this almost universal response stems from the years our ancestors spent on the savannas in Africa.[1]

People think using pictures. John Berger, media theorist, writes in his book *Ways of Seeing* (Penguin Books, 1972), "Seeing comes before words ... The child looks and recognizes before it can speak." Dr. Lynell Burmark, Ph.D. Associate at the Thornburg Center for Professional Development and writer of several books and

QUICK NOTE

According to a study by the United States Armed Forces, 83% of what we learn is through our eyes.

*Dr. Mehrabian notes that the actual percentage varies situationally but nonverbal communication carries great weight.
1. Stevenson Johnson, "Beauty and the Beastly PC, The Graphics on Your Screen Can Affect the Way You Feel—and Think," *Discover* Volume 25: Number 5 (May 2004): 20-21.

papers on visual literacy, said, "… unless our words, concepts, ideas are hooked onto an image, they will go in one ear, sail through the brain, and go out the other ear. Words are processed by our short-term memory where we can only retain about 7 bits of information (plus or minus 2). This is why, by the way, that we have 7-digit phone numbers. Images, on the other hand, go directly into long-term memory where they are indelibly etched." Therefore, it is not surprising that it is much easier to show a circle than describe it.

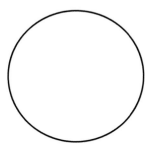

a curved line
with every point
equal distance
from the center

When it comes to quick, clear communication, visuals trump text almost every time. Presented with the following textual and visual information, are you afraid to pet this dog?

The very same visual elements that we are indelibly drawn to and so quickly absorb not only communicate data more efficiently and effectively but also affect us emotionally. For instance, research shows exposure to the color red can heighten our pulse and breathing rates.

What is your reaction to the picture on the left? How do you feel when you look at this picture? How quickly did you feel that way? Can you see how this image could be used to immediately elicit a strong emotional response and influence the viewer? If I were to textually describe this picture, your emotional reaction would not be as strong, and it would take more time for you to digest the information. J. Francis Davis, an adult educator and media education specialist, captured it well when he said, "… in our culture pictures have become tools used to elicit specific and planned emotional reactions in the people who see them." Visuals are not only excellent communicators but also quickly affect us psychologically and physiologically.

Don Norman, author of *Emotional Design,* said in a *Discover* magazine article, "Beauty and the Beastly PC: The Graphics on Your Computer Screen Can Affect the Way You Feel—and Think,"

> "I started out as an engineer, and I thought that what was really important was that something worked. Appearance—how could that matter? And yet for some reason, I would still buy attractive things, even if they didn't work as well as the less attractive ones. This puzzled me. In the last two years, I've finally come to understand that it's a result of the extremely tight coupling between emotion and cognition. Emotion is about judging the world, and cognition is about understanding. They can't be separated."

How many times have you heard, "I didn't believe it until I saw it." Studies show that the old saying "seeing is believing" is mostly true. Of course, we know that what we see can be manipulated, but the point is that visuals are persuasive. The Stanford Persuasive Technology Lab asked 2,440 participants how they evaluated the credibility of websites they were shown. Almost half (46.1%) said the website's design (color, graphics, layout, etc.) was the number one criterion for discerning the *credibility* of the presented material. The following are some of the captured participant comments:

> "This site is more credible. I find it to be much more professional looking." — M, 38, Washington

> "More pleasing graphics, higher-quality look and feel …" — F, 52, Tennessee

> "Just looks more credible." — M, 24, New Jersey

> "I know this is superficial, but the first thing that struck me is the color difference. The … site is a soothing green (sort of like money) while the [other] site is a jarring purple." — M, 56, Virginia

The ability of visual stimuli to communicate and influence is undeniable and inescapable. Through evolution, human beings are compelled to view and disseminate visuals. Recognizing the importance of visual communication is key to your success. Allen Ginsberg, poet and author, stated, "Whoever controls the media—the images—controls the culture." As early as the late nineteenth century, advertisers, based on their collective experience, were convinced that illustrations sold goods. World War II propaganda posters were very effective at manipulating popular opinion.

QUICK NOTE

"Patrick Renvoise, cofounder of SalesBrain, LLC and co-author of *Neuro-marketing: Is There a "Buy Button" in the Brain? Selling to the Old Brain for Instant Success,* says we should rethink marketing to reflect current brain understanding. To start with, marketing should be more visual and less verbal. Areas of the brain are much older than those of language, Renvoise says. That has implications for anyone attempting to influence decision makers. 'A lot of entrepreneurs talk about their benefit or solution and don't use a strong visual metaphor,' Renvoise says. 'And it's very hard to convince people using words when their organ of decision is primarily vision.'"

(Mark Henricks, "Gray Matters," *Entrepreneur* [January 2005]: 70-73)

(left) Grigware, Edward T. "Keep mum - the world has ears." By the People, For the People: Posters from the WPA, 1936-1943 from the Library of Congress. [http://hdl.loc.gov/loc.pnp/cph.3f05554] [cph 3f05554] (January 8, 2005). (right) Crandell, Bradshaw, "Are you a girl with star-spangled heart?" By the People, For the People: Posters from the WPA, 1936-1943 from the Library of Congress. [http://hdl.loc.gov/loc.pnp/cph.3g01653] [cph 3g01653] (January 8, 2005).

QUICK NOTE

"John Phillip Jones, a professor of advertising at Syracuse University in New York, says that the brain studies suggest that most ads need emotional appeal to get people to pay attention long enough to get in the rational selling proposition."

(Mark Henricks, "Gray Matters," *Entrepreneur* [January 2005]: 70-73)

The Sunday *New York Times* published "Good as a Gun: When Cameras Define a War," an article that effectively dealt with how the images photojournalists capture have influenced world affairs. Despite the best efforts of politicians, commanders, generals, and others involved with the war efforts, it was imagery that became the catalyst for some of the most pronounced changes. Reading or hearing about a situation is very different from seeing it.

In 1986, a 3M-sponsored study at the University of Minnesota School of Management found that **presenters who use visual aids are 43% more effective in persuading audience members to take a desired course of action** than presenters who don't use visuals. The goal of the experiment was to persuade undergraduates to commit their time and money to attending time management seminars. Presenters of various skill levels participated. Researchers found that average presenters who used visual aids were as effective as more advanced presenters using no visuals. In addition, the study found that the audience *expected* the advanced presenters to include professional, quality visuals. What about you? Have you noticed the increase in visual aids during presentations? Do you prefer presentations with or without visuals?[2]

Human communication has existed for about 30,000 years. In the beginning of recorded history, the vast majority of what we communicated was not text based.[3] Textual communication has been with us in one form or another for only 3,700 years. With the invention of tools like Gutenberg's movable type printing press in 1450, text took center stage. Graphics were too costly to include. As printing costs dropped, graphics soon resurfaced and their frequency is rising. In 1995, Charles Brumback, the chairman of the Newspaper Association of America, said, "as newspaper penetration falls … the culture itself moves from textual to visual

2. (Reworded but from) Jon Hanke, *The Psychology of Presentation Visuals*, www.presentations.com.
3. Duncan Davies, Diana Bathurst, and Robin Bathurst, *The Telling Image The Changing Balance between Pictures and Words in a Technological Age* (Oxford: Clarendon Press, 1990).

INTRODUCTION: THE POWER OF GRAPHICS

literacy."[4] Gunther Kress is a Professor of English and Education at the School of Education, University of London. His research confirms this changeover. As an example, Kress compares science textbooks from 1936 and 1988 showing that textbooks have progressed from a majority of text to a majority of graphics.[5]

The change isn't limited to textbooks and newspapers. Signs, maps, instructions, schematics, icons, symbols, and packaging sell products, warn of possible hazards, and give visual direction when words alone are not sufficient. Graphics are found on websites, TV shows, appliances, and computers; in vehicles and books; and at museums, malls, restaurants, and grocery stores. More and more professions that rely heavily on communication and persuasion are embracing graphics as a tool of choice. In the *Boston Globe* article, "Courtroom Graphics Come of Cyber-Age," author Sacha Pfeiffer found that "… new technologies—and a new willingness in legal circles to embrace them—have taken the use of visual images in the courtroom to a level unimaginable even a decade ago … The result is a slow but significant shift in the way many trial lawyers, who historically have relied largely on their verbal skills to sway juries, try cases … More prosecutors see high-tech graphics not as a luxury, but as a necessity."

Graphic communication is more ubiquitous than ever before. Why? Because graphics do what text alone cannot do. They *quickly* affect us both cognitively and emotionally:

1) **Cognitively**: Graphics expedite and increase our level of communication. They increase comprehension, recollection, and retention. Visual clues help us decode text and attract attention to information or direct attention increasing the likelihood that the audience will remember.[6]

2) **Emotionally**: Pictures enhance or affect emotions and attitudes.[7] Graphics engage our imagination and heighten our creative thinking by stimulating other areas of our brain (which in turn leads to a more profound and accurate understanding of the presented material).[8] It is no secret that emotions influence decision-making:

> "(Emotions) play an essential role in decision making, perception, learning, and more … they influence the very mechanisms of rational thinking."[9]

4. M. Fitzgerald, "NAA Leaders Disagree Over Value Cyberspace," *International Federation of Newspaper Publishers Research Association* 128(12) (1995): 48-49.

5. "'English' at the Crossroads: Rethinking Curricula of Communication in the Context of a Turn to the Visual"

6. W.H. Levie and R. Lentz, "Effects of Text Illustrations: A Review of Research," *Educational Communications and Technology Journal* 30 (4) (1982): 195-232.

7. W.H. Levie and R. Lentz, "Effects of Text Illustrations: A Review of Research," *Educational Communications and Technology Journal* 30 (4) (1982): 195-232.

8. D. Bobrow and D. Norman, "Some Principles of Memory Schemata," (in D. Bobrow and A.Collins [eds.]), *Representation and Understanding: Studies in Cognitive Science* (New York: Academic Press, 1975): 131-149. *and* D. Rumelhart, "Schemata: The Building Blocks of Cognition," (in R.J. Spiro, B.C. Bruce and W.F. Brewer [eds.]), *Theoretical Issues in Reading Comprehension* (Hillsdale, New Jersey: Lawrence Erlbaum Associate, 1980), 33-58.

9. H. van Oostendorp, J. Preece and A.G. Arnold (guest editorial), "Designing Multimedia for Human Needs and Capabilities," *Interacting with Computers* Volume 12, Issue 1 (September 1999): 1-5.

QUICK NOTE

The motion picture industry uses storyboards or animatics to tell the story prior to filming. Actions, framing, pacing, lighting, and a host of critical details are communicated to the production crew and actors using storyboards and animatics.

Behavioral Psychologists agree that most of our decisions are based on intuitive judgment and emotions. Herbert A. Simon, Nobel Prize winning scholar at the Carnegie Mellon Institute in Pittsburgh, studied corporate decision-making and found that people often ignored formal decision-making models because of time constraints, incomplete information, the inability to calculate consequences, and other variables. Intuitive judgment was the process for most decisions. Neurologist Antonio Damasio studied research on patients with damaged ventromedial frontal cortices of the brain, which impaired their ability to feel but left their ability to think analytically intact. Damasio discovered that the patients were unable to make rational decisions even though their ability to reason was fully functional. He concluded that reasoning "depends, to a considerable extent, on a continual ability to experience feelings."[10]

Psychologists Amos Twersky and Nobel Prize winner Daniel Kahnerman demonstrated that decision-making also depended on how the problems were framed or described, which results in predictable cognitive patterns and errors in judgment. Consider the following example:

"A bat and a ball cost $1.10 in total. The bat costs $1 more than the ball. How much does the ball cost?"[10]

The question is asked in a way that clouds the correct answer. If the question were worded as follows:

A bat and a ball cost $1.10 in total. The bat cost $1.05. How much does the ball cost?

The answer would be obvious: 5¢. Much as phraseology influences the response to a question, how and what you show influences the audience's response.

WHO IS SMARTER? WHICH IS BETTER?

10. Jayme A. Sokolow, "How Do Reviewers Really Evaluate Your Proposal? What the Cognitive Science of Heuristics Tells Us About Making Decisions," *Journal of the Association of Proposal Management Professionals* (Spring/Summer 2004): 34-50.

So visuals are processed 60,000 times faster than text, graphics quickly affect our emotions, and our emotions greatly affect our decision-making. If most of our decisions are based on relatively quick intuitional judgment and emotions, then how many decisions are influenced by visually appealing, easily digested graphics? The answer is no secret to advertisers.

Billions of dollars are spent annually to find the right imagery to sell a product, service, or idea. The U.S. military spent $598 million in 2003 on advertising to increase "brand identity" and meet their annual recruitment goals. Nike spent $269 million in 2001 on its image to sell more products. Anheuser-Busch spent $440 million to promote its products in 2001. Pepsi budgeted over $1 billion in 2001 on its image. Not to be outdone, Coca-Cola budgeted $1.4 billion for its image in the same year. Graphics help create "brand identity." Visuals paint the picture of who the advertiser is, what they stand for, and how the audience may benefit. Graphics sell because of their ability to influence. How you use graphics greatly affects how you and your business are perceived.

Study after study, experiment after experiment has proven graphics have immense influence over the audience's perception of the subject matter and, by association, the presenter (the person, place, or thing most associated with the graphic) because of these neurological and evolutionary factors. The audience's understanding of the presented material, opinion of the presented material and the presenter, and their emotional state are crucial factors in any decision they will make. Without a doubt, **graphics greatly influence an audience's decisions.** Whoever properly wields this intelligence has a powerful advantage over their competition.

Larry Tracy, who now trains corporate executives to make oral presentations for government contracts, headed the Pentagon's top briefing team and worked for years with the Department of State. He was aware that graphics were so influential in the government's decision to purchase goods and services that bad buying decisions were made based on the quality of the visuals in the presented materials. This has in turn led to the government, at times, putting constraints on presented graphics by requiring black and white submissions or even requiring that no graphics be used in a presentation to reduce the likelihood of high-quality, polished graphics unfairly persuading evaluators.

I spent many years analyzing how the proposal industry works (an industry that focuses on the submission of written and oral presentations to secure work that will increase or maintain a company's revenue). I found that the priority of graphic development increases as award value rises. This industry understands the influence that graphics have on their audience. It is common knowledge to companies like Northrop Grumman, Raytheon, Boeing, and Lockheed Martin that graphics are an essential part of winning new government business. In fact, it is not uncommon, when exceptional graphics are used, for government evaluators to commend the presenter on their use of graphics.

QUICK NOTE

According to studies performed at the Wharton School at the University of Pennsylvania, the University of Minnesota Management Information Systems Research Center, and 3M:

- People agree more with a position when presented with visuals.

- People will pay closer attention and react more positively when visuals are used.

- The quality of a meeting is increased by the use of visuals.

QUICK NOTE

"'Fifteen years ago, companies competed on price. Today it's quality. Tomorrow it's design.'—Bob Hayes, professor emeritus at Harvard Business School"

(Tom Peters, *Design* [DK Publishing, Inc., 2005])

Flags, eagles, and other symbols of patriotism are often included on proposal covers simply because of the positive emotional influence patriotic imagery has on government evaluators. Part of the cover's goal is to instantly establish that the presenter is a supportive, trustworthy, reliable patriot. As a result, the government evaluator is more likely to be in a positive, agreeable state of mind when reading the proposal. As stated earlier, emotions influence the very mechanisms of rational thinking, so if the evaluator's mood is elevated by the visuals, the more likely he or she is to agree with the presenter.

 QUICK NOTE

Although infrequently, proposals have been won and lost because of covers. A well-designed cover that focuses on the costumer's benefits or addresses key issues plays a substantial role in the final decision.

I am not saying that graphic communication is better than text. The combination of graphics and words has a communicative power that neither singularly possesses.

> "Pictures interact with text to produce levels of comprehension and memory that can exceed what is produced by text alone."[11]

Without graphics, an idea may be lost in a sea of words. Without words, a graphic may be lost to ambiguity. Robert E. Horn, an award-winning scholar at Stanford University's Center for the Study of Language and Information, said, "When words and visual elements are closely entwined, we create something new and we augment our communal intelligence ... visual language has the potential for increasing 'human bandwidth'—the capacity to take in, comprehend, and more efficiently synthesize large amounts of new information."

Our communication paradigm is evolving.

11. J.R. Levin, A Transfer of Appropriate Processing Perspective of Pictures in Prose, (in H.Mandl and J.R. Levin [eds.]) *Knowledge Acquisition from Text and Prose* (Amsterdam: ElsevierScience Publishers, 1989).

CHAPTER 1:
THE LIFECYCLE OF A
SUCCESSFUL GRAPHIC

There are two tiers of communication for all graphics: **Surface (Cognitive)** and **Subsurface (Emotional)**.

SURFACE (COGNITIVE)

Surface communication is the cognitive process surrounding reading, understanding, and/or learning from the information presented. In other words, it is the graphic's ability to communicate information that is consistent with your primary objective, such as selling a product or service.

All visuals communicate information:

- A logo communicates the presenter's identity or information about a presenter's product or service.
- A photograph communicates the styling of a new car or the look of a new jacket.
- A book cover communicates the subject matter of a book.
- Assembly instructions communicate how to put a bookshelf together.
- A process diagram conveys the review process of an evaluation committee or an overview of how binary code is processed.

SUBSURFACE (EMOTIONAL)

Subsurface communication is the subconscious effect a graphic and its content has on our emotional state—our state of mind.

Many visuals are designed to affect us emotionally. According to independent research, everything we see elicits an emotional response that affects our state of mind—whether we realize it or not. Many graphics harness this aspect of human perception in an effort to influence and motivate the audience. For example, pictures of beautiful people sell us handbags, images of starving children plead with us to donate money, patriotic pictures instill trust and influence us to join the military, even the use of the color red quickens our pulse and influences our mood.

Surface and subsurface communication are tightly linked. Each affects the other. All surface and subsurface data interact to form a cohesive picture of the

QUICK NOTE

Using visuals in a presentation

- ... improved learning 200%
  —*University of Wisconsin*

- ... took 40% less time
  to explain complex ideas
  —*Wharton School*

- ... improved retention 38%
  —*Harvard University*

QUICK NOTE

Jin Woo Kim, professor at Yonsei University, and Jae Yun Moon, assistant professor at Hong Kong University of Science and Technology, found that manipulating visual design factors could induce a target emotion such as trustworthiness.

(J. Kim and J.Y. Moon, "Designing Towards Emotional Usability in Customer Interfaces—Trustworthiness of Cyber-banking System Interfaces," *Interacting with Computers* Volume 10: Issue 1 (March 1998): 1-29)

presenter and their offerings to the audience. Assuming no other input, these elements combine to create the audience's lasting impression of the presenter and ultimately results in a final judgment.

In the world of visual communication there are two principal needs:

1) **Communicate information**

2) **Influence or motivate the audience**

Aside from those graphics used for pure statistical analysis of empirical data, almost all graphics are influencing the audience to agree with the presenter and arrive at an intended conclusion. It is the intent of the conceptualizer that determines the extent to which subsurface communication is utilized to achieve the primary objective.

A **successful** graphic should answer the audience's questions. It should answer the audience's who, what, where, when, why, and/or how questions. Since *everything* we see elicits an emotional response that affects our state of mind, the graphic will also communicate other, less identifiable, subsurface ideas such as the credibility, competency, professionalism, reliability, creativity, and strength of the presenter. Your goal is to elicit emotions in the audience that support the author's and presenter's goals.

The following process helps guarantee a successful graphic:

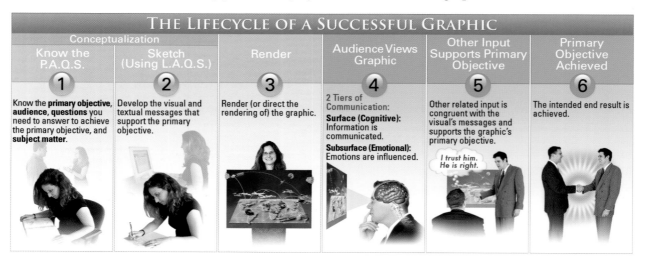

STEP 1—KNOW THE P.A.Q.S. Know the primary objective, audience, questions to which the audience wants answered to achieve the primary objective, and subject matter. Knowing your audience is key. Know their buzzwords, their likes, and their dislikes. Know exactly what you want to say and why it matters to your audience.

STEP 2—CONCEPTUALIZE YOUR GRAPHIC. Use the four methods, thirteen design techniques, and twelve techniques for affecting emotions found later in this book to quickly turn any idea into a clear, communicative, compelling visual.

STEP 3—RENDER YOUR GRAPHIC (or direct the rendering of your graphic). Be sure your image is rendered the *right* way. Your graphic should be clean, concise, aesthetically appealing, error free, and rendered in a style faithful to the subject matter and your audience. (You will learn the secrets in Chapters 3 and 4.)

When it is time to present your visual, your graphic has only one other hurdle to jump before accomplishing its primary objective: outside influences. Unfortunately, there are other less controllable and accountable elements that determine audience acceptance. An example is a technical glitch like the loss of power or a computer malfunction. Your graphic's success is contingent upon the audience's

- perception (factual or not) of the presenter, the material, and the environment
- biases
- life experience
- open mindedness
- intelligence
- comfort
- state of mind

Consider the following two scenarios:

Scenario 1: A professionally designed, factually accurate PowerPoint presentation contains your graphic. Unfortunately, the oral presenter is disheveled and dressed inappropriately, wearing a t-shirt, shorts, and sneakers. The presenter's appearance distracts the audience from the material. Whether your graphic is perceived as credible and factual is now in question.

Scenario 2: Due to past experience, the audience is biased against the presenter. They may have experienced poor customer service or once owned a defective product made by the presenter's company. Acceptance may not occur.

The court system is a perfect example of an industry that mitigates the potential risk of outside influences. Attorneys, aware of the damage preexisting prejudices may have, prepare special questions to weed out jurors who may cost them the win. For high profile cases, chosen jurors are often sequestered to avoid the likelihood that outside influences will affect their decisions.

Controllable elements (data accuracy, spelling, room temperature) as well as outside influences (unintended associations, unexpected technical glitches) can determine whether or not your graphic is given the positive attention it requires to succeed. For this reason, take into account as many variables as possible

QUICK NOTE

"Speak, not so that you may be understood, but so that you cannot be misunderstood."
–Quintilian

during the creation and presentation of your graphic. The goal is that everything associated with your graphic is congruent with its primary objective.

It is not necessary for one person to perform all of the steps involved to create a successful graphic. **The entire process can be collaborative.** For example, one person may have customer insight, another may be a subject matter expert, while others may hold the remaining pieces of the puzzle. Together they may possess the necessary knowledge to produce a successful graphic.

Your visual depictions are limited only by your (or your group's) imagination and the audience's understanding of the visual representation you choose. Be creative and have fun.

CHAPTER 2:
STEP 1—KNOW THE P.A.Q.S.

First, know what you wish to accomplish. What is your PRIMARY OBJECTIVE (P)? In a perfect world, what would the audience do or think after viewing your graphic?

Second, know your AUDIENCE (A). Know who they are, what they want to see, and why they should care. Learn what your audience truly desires. Your target audience is the sole reason why you are creating your visual. Tailor your graphic to your target audience. Make sure your audience can see themselves in your graphic. Connect with their world.

Third, know (and answer) the QUESTIONS (Q) to which your audience needs answers so that your graphic can achieve its primary objective. Put yourself in their shoes. What would you want to know to move forward? What is it about your graphic that helps your audience? Make it obvious. Highlight your features, benefits, and discriminators. Focus on the audience's wants and needs.

Fourth, know the SUBJECT MATTER (S). How could you answer the audience's questions without an understanding of the presented topic? The more you understand your subject matter, the more likely your graphic will be successful.

Knowing your P.A.Q.S. is vital to the success of your graphic. Finding this information is 50% of the conceptualization process. Without it, you are conceptualizing in the dark.

QUICK NOTE

Legendary philosopher Harry Overstreet wrote in *Influencing Human Behavior,* "Action springs out of what we fundamentally desire."

THE PRIMARY OBJECTIVE

Know the primary objective of your graphic. The primary objective is the goal or the conclusion at which your audience arrives after viewing your graphic. It is the purpose for which you created your graphic. Your goal may be to simply share information, sell a product or service, explain quantum physics, or help someone navigate the streets of the city as easily as possible. Every graphic has a primary objective.

Your primary objective determines your content. For example, the objective of your graphic might be to convince your audience that a new process for employee orientation is better than the old process. This objective would govern what information you include in your visual.

To establish the primary objective you need to understand the purpose your graphic serves. Essentially, ask yourself, "So what? Why does your audience care?" Once you determine its purpose, there are two possible paths you can choose when developing your graphic:

1) **Communicate information.** (Your goal is to explain or clarify *only*. Influencing your audience is not the focus.)

2) **Influence or motivate.** (Includes the explanation or clarification needed to persuade your audience.)

Communicate Information

If your goal is to communicate information, your primary objective is to share facts that educate your audience. The following are examples of primary objectives that explain or clarify and the associated graphic.

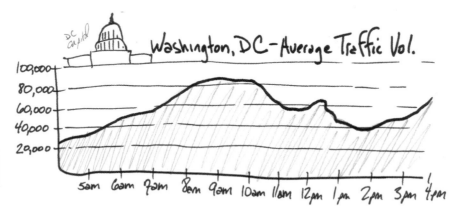

PRIMARY OBJECTIVE (COMMUNICATE INFORMATION): Communicate aggregate traffic volume in Washington, D.C.

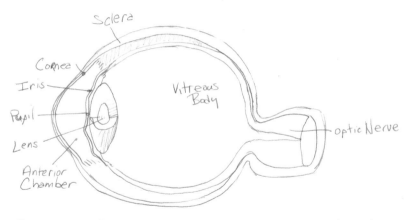

PRIMARY OBJECTIVE (COMMUNICATE INFORMATION): Explain the structure of the human eye.

PRIMARY OBJECTIVE (COMMUNICATE INFORMATION): Explain the roles and responsibilities of four different companies working together.

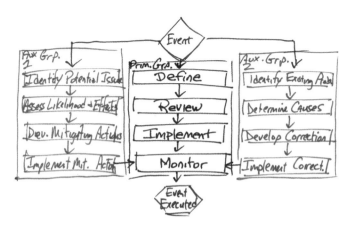

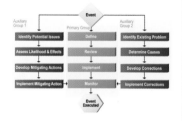

PRIMARY OBJECTIVE (COMMUNICATE INFORMATION): Explain the problem resolution process.

Influence or Motivate

If your goal is to influence or motivate, **your primary objective must include a benefit and how the benefit will be accomplished.** (The "how" can be a discriminator when appropriate.) In business, it is *often* the case that the goal is to persuade. Most authors of graphics fall prey to misunderstanding the true purpose of their graphic. They forget to see it from their audience's perspective. The following example shows how to turn a bad primary objective into an excellent primary objective where the goal is to influence.

BAD PRIMARY OBJECTIVE (INFLUENCE OR MOTIVATE): **Show our new network's architecture.**

Ask yourself, "So what? What does your audience *really* want from your solution?" Let's say your audience wants to lower their cost, increase their network's speed, and eliminate network downtime. Your primary objective must show how these benefits will be achieved through the solution you present. Your primary objective must have a benefit and explain the how. Think of your primary objective as the "**takeaway**" or conclusion.

GOOD PRIMARY OBJECTIVE (INFLUENCE OR MOTIVATE): Lower cost, increased speed, and greater uptime are ensured through our three-step network approach.

Notice that the revised primary objective places the benefits *first*, which gives your audience a reason to care. Next, the primary objective briefly explains how the benefits will be achieved. (Your graphic must further explain the how.)

The resulting graphics from these two primary objectives are dramatically different.

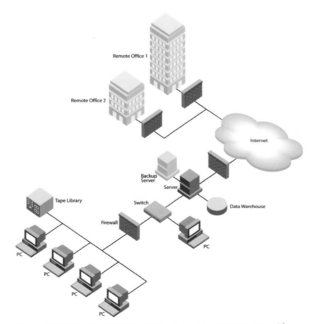

BAD PRIMARY OBJECTIVE (INFLUENCE OR MOTIVATE): **Show our new network's architecture.**

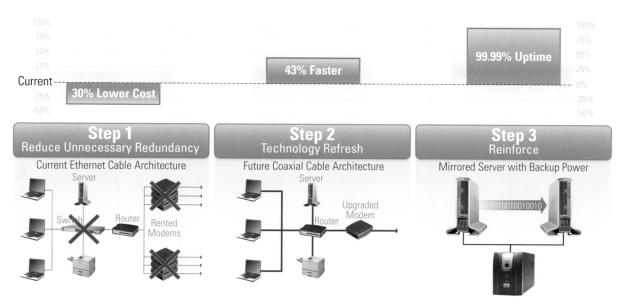

GOOD PRIMARY OBJECTIVE (INFLUENCE OR MOTIVATE): Lower cost, increased speed, and greater uptime are ensured through our three-step network approach.

If your goal is to influence or motivate, focus on the benefit of your idea, product, or service to your audience. Do not be vague. Every company says their solution is better, faster, cheaper, and offers more value than the alternative. Be specific. Link a feature with the benefit to your audience, so they will care (e.g., our computer uses the new X20 processor, which is 100% faster, so you can get your work done twice as fast).

People don't buy features, they buy the resulting benefits of those features. Imagine walking into a car dealership and the salesperson exclaims, "Wow, you picked the best day to buy a new Honda Accord. We just added the 323i engine!" You shrug and ask, "What is the deal with the 323i engine?" He replies, "The 323i engine gets 75 miles per gallon and accelerates from 0-60 miles per hour in 3.2 seconds." *Now* you care about the 323i engine. You are interested because he linked a feature to a benefit.

Your audience takes notice and begins to care if they know and understand the benefits. If you can save your audience time and money, fulfill a pressing need, or reduce hassle and make their lives easier, show it in your graphic. The more your target audience cares, the more attention is given to the graphic and the more likely it is that your graphic succeeds. The audience will not care about your product or service if the focus is not on them and their wants and needs. If you can show that your quick service will save them 30% or $140,000 per year over their current service, then they will listen and care. Solve their problem. Show the benefits that they will enjoy. Help them become enthusiastic about the subject and the prospect of having, using, or implementing it. If the benefit is not blindingly obvious, make it crystal clear.

QUICK NOTE

The simpler the primary objective, the more powerful the graphic. Adding more benefits dilutes any one benefit. For example, it is more memorable to say that your solution lowers cost rather than lowers cost, risk, and increases speed.

QUICK NOTE

Graphic titles (the text that names and explains your graphic) or presentation "takeaways" (the text that sums up your slide) is your primary objective. Your graphic must prove or support that statement.

In the next graphic, the ONGO Quality Council uses engineering, testing, and integration to guarantee continual improvement.

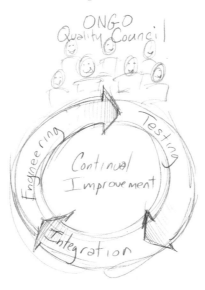

So what? If the primary objective of this graphic is to show what elements come together into one seamless process to guarantee continual improvement, it is acceptable as is. On the other hand, what if the primary objective is to show how the ONGO Quality Council's process benefits the audience?

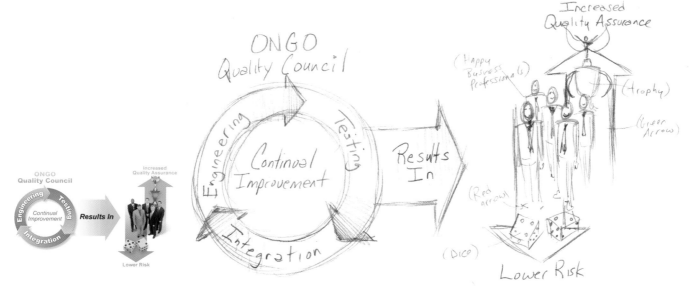

Now the graphic addresses why the process should matter to the audience. It shows that the ONGO Quality Council uses engineering, testing, and integration to guarantee continual improvement, which results in lower risk, increased quality assurance, and a happy client.

The following graphics communicate the benefits of a solution to positively influence the audience.

PRIMARY OBJECTIVE (INFLUENCE OR MOTIVATE): A winning team is the result of eight critical elements.

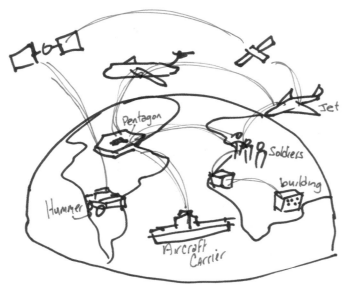

PRIMARY OBJECTIVE (INFLUENCE OR MOTIVATE): Communicate with anyone, anywhere using our solution.

THE AUDIENCE

Have you heard someone use an acronym you did not know? How about a new slang term that was baffling? Were you ever lost while learning something new? How did it make you feel? To misunderstand or struggle with new information can be frustrating. It results in a host of negative feelings. For this reason, **know your audience.**

Who will be viewing this graphic? What language do they speak? What are their *buzz words?* What are their *hot buttons?* What do they like/dislike (colors, imagery, detailed explanations, etc.)? What do they **really** want from this transaction (to work less, more free time, more money)? If you don't know much about your audience, find out! Ask them questions. Research their organization. Visit their website. Talk with those who know them better than you such as current or former employees or their clients. Without an understanding of the audience, you will not know what they want and need and how best to communicate that information. The more insight you have into your audience, the greater your chances for achieving your primary objective.

You must know your target audience. If I try to sell you home remodeling when you are looking for a new home, I will fail no matter how enticing my graphic. Without insight into your audience, how can you know what they really want?

For example, which of the following slides would be more communicative to the United States Army (A or B)?

The presenter of slide (A) focuses on the target audience. Slide (A) uses terms and imagery to which the U.S. Army can understand and relate. It addresses issues the Army cares about. The likelihood that the slide will clearly communicate the intended messages significantly increases. Slide (B) is focused on the presenter and what they want to say about themselves without regard to their audience.

The presenter of slide Ⓑ failed to learn more about the target audience and the slide reflects that fact. They present slide Ⓑ as if they were presenting to another business within their industry instead of catering to the potential client.

Let your audience see themselves in your visuals. If your target audience is parents, show images of families. If your goal is to win a contract from the Army, use Army specific imagery. Developing a graphic that reaches the audience on a personal level involves research and an understanding of your target audience's desires and challenges.

I work for many government contracting companies that develop great insight into their potential clients. For example, Company A may hire a former employee of the Department of Defense (DoD) for which they are trying to work. Hiring a former DoD employee gives them an insider's understanding of DoD's operating procedures, budget constraints, power struggles, needs, wants, and challenges. Alternatively, Company A may submit an unsolicited proposal because, during a preexisting project with the DoD, Company A saw an opportunity to improve the DoD's operations. Company A can leverage their existing relationship and understanding of their client against their client's current needs to create a focused, compelling, timely presentation. Using their knowledge of the DoD, Company A has the upper hand over any competitor.

Understanding your audience is critical. One of my associates created software to manage her company's digital assets. Unfortunately, she encountered problems with the tool she created and soon realized that she needed to hire an outside firm to create a better solution. Only one person bidding on the opportunity was wise enough to talk with her and learn that the new proposed solution must not negatively reference her existing tool. If the bidder criticized the asset management tool she created, it would reflect poorly on her and may result in a demotion. Guess which bidder she chose?

 QUICK NOTE

If your target audience calls a "widget" a "wodget," then you call it a "wodget" as well. (You can educate your audience on the proper term after they choose your solution.)

THE QUESTIONS

You might be surprised at the number of graphics that fail because the information presented ignored the primary objective, the audience, and their questions. The author of the visual did not have a clear idea of what they wanted to communicate and what their audience wanted to know. Typically, an author tries to communicate too many one-sided messages through one visual. The resulting graphic is unsightly, hard to read, fails to communicate the intended information, and doesn't answer the audience's questions. How do you avoid creating a graphic that fails to communicate the right information? **Know the questions your audience needs answered so your graphic can achieve its primary objective.**

To begin developing your questions, discern the number one question to which your audience wants an answer before they can move forward. What is the most important point to be communicated by the graphic that supports the primary objective? Then, when applicable, figure out the secondary and tertiary questions that support the primary objective. Put yourself in your audience's position. What would you want to know to make a buying decision or find value in the presented information? You want answers to questions like who, what, where, when, why, or how. You may want answers to the following questions:

- Why should I care?
- What is it?
- What does it do?
- How does it work?
- How much does it cost?
- How fast is it?
- How long does it take?
- What makes it better than anything else?

Often, when the goal is to influence or motivate, authors of graphics develop questions that are unrelated to the primary objective or are focused on minutia. To avoid writing the wrong questions, I recommend the following exercise: Imagine pitching your solution to a decision maker at a networking event. Your pitch is your primary objective. What follow-up questions would they ask? For example, you state, "You can save $20,000 per year with Connetix, the best automated tracking tool on the market." The decision maker may ask these questions:

1) What makes it the best?
2) How will it save me $20,000 per year?
3) How much does it cost?

Create a list of **up to five questions** the graphic must answer to achieve the primary objective. Focus on only the most important questions otherwise you may sacrifice clarity, which usually results in the graphic's failure. Odds are good (unless your audience is focused on technical data only) that the decision maker will not ask questions focused on the smallest details like, "Is Connetix written using PHP3 with NTR backbone?" Their questions will always be short and simple because they want to quickly decide if you are wasting their time.

There may be other questions the decision maker might ask. If a follow up question is of great importance to them, it needs to become a standalone graphic. For example, the decision maker may ask, "How will it work with my current systems?" The answer to this question would become a new primary objective for an additional graphic.

Make it easy for your audience to find the answers they seek. For example, the graphic below helps the buyer quickly choose the best television.

Of course, to answer your audience's questions you **must** understand your subject matter, which brings us to the next section.

THE SUBJECT MATTER

Know your subject matter. To correctly answer your audience's questions, you need a clear understanding of the presented topic. If *you* do not understand, how can your audience understand?

I conceptualized the next graphic for a presentation to provide help desk support. The graphic's primary objective was to communicate the functional architecture of the help desk solution. I asked questions about the primary objective and the target audience. Based on that insight, I determined the questions to which the audience would want answers:

1) What are the benefits of using a new architecture?
2) How does it work? (How do the pieces fit together?)
3) What is unique about the solution?
4) Can it work with legacy systems?

To conceptualize a graphic that answered these questions, I needed to understand the help desk solution. I asked the subject matter experts these four questions. I continued to ask more questions until I had a clear understanding of the answers. I listened attentively and recorded what I learned.

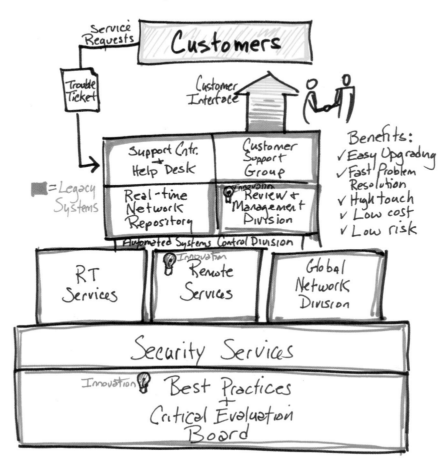

The following image identifies all questions and answers.

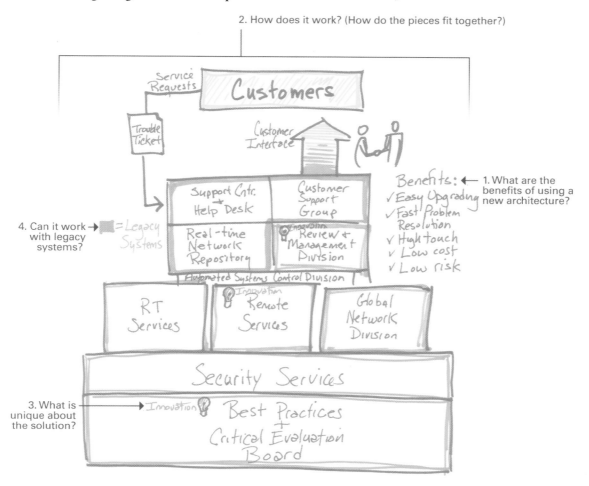

It is essential to adequately understand the information you are conveying and how best to relate it to your audience's needs. How likely is it that the graphic will be successful if you, the conceptualizer, do not understand the subject matter and how it is relevant to the audience?

Ensure your knowledge of the subject matter is accurate. If you misunderstand your subject matter, your answers will be misleading. If your information is incorrect or inaccurate, your graphic will fail and reflect negatively on anyone or anything associated with it. Even worse, your audience may feel lied to—no one trusts a liar. Once the audience believes the data is false or the presenter is misleading, trust is broken, and lack of trust causes the validity of your graphic to be questioned. If you do not properly research the subject and you present inaccurate or dated information, then the credibility of the graphic will be nullified and not accepted by your target audience.

For example, a mall kiosk contains a map that has not been updated with a jewelry store's replacement by sporting goods store. Anyone who uses the map

 QUICK NOTE

If you do not know the answers to the questions and have no access to a subject matter expert, research your answers carefully. Never present unsubstantiated information.

to find the jewelry store is frustrated. The validity of the map is questioned. The mall-goer's perception of the mall's ability to serve their needs is negatively affected.

I worked for a trial support firm. The job of my colleagues and I was to create graphics that illustrated mechanisms, machines, and processes for patent law cases. It was imperative that the graphics were accurate. If the opposing legal team called our visuals into question, revealing misleading or false data, the case could be lost. It was of the utmost importance that the graphics supported the court's opinion that our client, the defendant, was honest and trustworthy.

Make sure your understanding of the subject matter is accurate and relevant to your audience's needs to help guarantee a successful graphic.

P.A.Q.S. Questionnaire

The following graphic summarizes the conceptualization process. Use it as a reminder when developing future graphics.

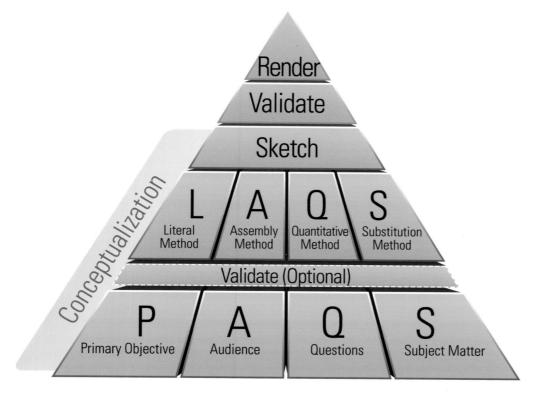

1) What is the **primary objective?**

(What is the goal? What is the conclusion or takeaway? Think about it from your audience's perspective. The primary objective must be no longer than one sentence and often includes a benefit and/or discriminator and how the benefit is achieved.)

> *Example: To show our client will lower their repair cost, repair time, and risk by using our new parts inventory review process.*

2) Who is your target **audience?**

(Know your audience. What do they care about/want to know?)

> *Example: This is for the U.S. Army vehicle part storage and repair facilities managers and their staff. They use the review process to make sure they have the most up-to-date parts list, so they have the parts they need when repairs are needed. Used to order new parts and track down missing parts.*

3) What audience **questions** (Q) must be answered to achieve the primary objective, and what are the answers (know your **subject matter [S]**) to those questions?

(Up to five questions relevant to the primary objective. Questions often include who, what, why, when, where, and how.)

AUDIENCE'S QUESTIONS	YOUR ANSWERS
Example: What is different about the new process?	Newer, faster chip in server. Automated, simplified process (fewer steps).
Example: Why is it better?	Saves the Army at least $120,000/year on repair costs because of labor cost savings from inventory accuracy and automation. Accurate, up-to-date inventory coupled with faster processor results in shorter repair time. Ease of use (simplified process and user interface), automation, proven technology, and greater accuracy lowers the risk of failure.
Example: How does it work?	Site managers receive online accounts (so we know who enters what request). All information is instantly added to the searchable database. The software automatically detects anomalies and self corrects. Physical inventory is constantly scanned using RFID technology to ensure accuracy. Once shipped or used, the inventory is tracked and logged for future reference, if needed.
Example: Is it proven? (Is it risky?)	Yes, it is proven. In fact, the system is less risky than what is currently in place. The review process is simpler and the backend is the same (which is very stable) except for the new server chip, which has been used at other sites for seven months with zero failure.

4) (If applicable.) What is unique about you and/or presented material and what is the direct benefit to your audience for each of the discriminators?

(Point out important and relevant discriminators and their benefits in your graphic.)

DISCRIMINATOR	DIRECT BENEFIT
Example: We are the only company that can get new chips for the lowest price.	Saves the Army at least $20,000 on upgrade costs.

CHAPTER 3:
STEP 2—SKETCH

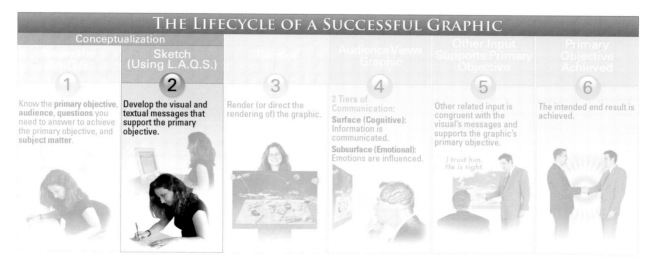

Now that you know your audience, what you want to say, and why it matters, it is time to do a very rough sketch of your graphic. No design skills are required. Sketches are often as simple as basic shapes or mock designs made in PowerPoint or other programs. (Label your elements to ensure your audience understands that your square represents a laptop or your smiley face represents a businessman at his desk.)

Focus on your graphic's ability to communicate. The core intent of most visuals is to transfer information from the graphic to its audience (no different than a written or oral explanation). You are communicating using a synthesis of graphics and text. Learning to do so is very similar to learning a new language. As with any new language, it can be difficult to communicate certain ideas and concepts. Do not get discouraged. You do it everyday but may fail to notice. In your routine activities, you often translate your verbal explanations into visual explanations. Watch people talk. Notice the ways in which their body language helps explain or clarify what they are saying. How many times have you said "let me show you" when words fail to effectively communicate? You are doing the same when conceptualizing a graphic. In a short time, it will be second nature.

The next three sections show you the three aspects of conceptualizing the clearest, most communicative, and compelling graphics possible.

First, you will learn the Four Methods. Second, you will learn how to illustrate repeatedly encountered concepts using simple design techniques. Lastly, you will understand when you should deliberately affect your audience's emotions and how to do it.

QUICK NOTE

Are you conceptualizing graphics for your marketing materials? There is one more method often applied to marketing design, the **Hyperbole Method**. Simply exaggerate your claim. For example, if an ad is touting a car's spaciousness it could show elephants, giraffes, basketball players, and other oversized objects entering the vehicle. The ad is visually overstating a claim to make a memorable point.

Four Methods

The Four Methods help you transform ideas, information, and data into powerful visuals. They are intuitive processes that are used independently or in conjunction with one another. The Four Methods are as follows:

1) **Literal Method:** Show exactly what is being described. Show the object, event, location, or process.

2) **Substitution Method:** Substitute or augment an image of one action, concept, or entity for another. Use imagery that is easy for the target audience to recognize and relate to and aids in the description or definition of the subject.

3) **Quantitative Method:** Use a quantitative graphic to quickly communicate and analyze amounts, time frames, or values. Quantitative graphics include area charts, bar charts, bubble charts, calendars, candlestick charts, circle charts, dashboards, Gantt charts, line charts, pie charts, point charts, tables, and timelines. (There are other quantitative graphic types but the types included in this book are more universally recognized and understood.)

4) **Assembly Method:** As you review the data to be visually depicted, capture important elements (ideas, concepts, actions, benefits, goals, departments, tasks, etc.) in blocks. Assemble these blocks in a manner that illustrates the "big picture." Arrange the boxes according to hierarchy, relationships, paths of communication, actions, and so on.

Let's explore each method ...

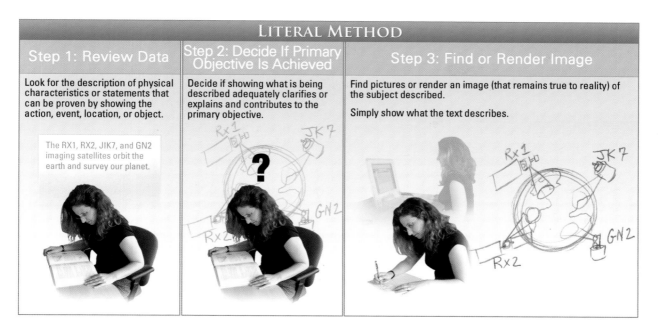

LITERAL METHOD

Step 1: Review Data	Step 2: Decide If Primary Objective Is Achieved	Step 3: Find or Render Image
Look for the description of physical characteristics or statements that can be proven by showing the action, event, location, or object.	Decide if showing what is being described adequately clarifies or explains and contributes to the primary objective.	Find pictures or render an image (that remains true to reality) of the subject described. Simply show what the text describes.

If "seeing is believing" and "a picture is worth a thousand words," the Literal Method is the pinnacle. Your resulting graphic is the equivalent of saying, "This is exactly what I mean."

Use the Literal Method to communicate what an object looks like, how to find your way, and how a product operates or is assembled. You can also use it to provide evidence of a stated attribute. For example, if the intent is to demonstrate a new Web portal's ease-of-use, show the new Web portal. It is a very effective way to substantiate the claim.

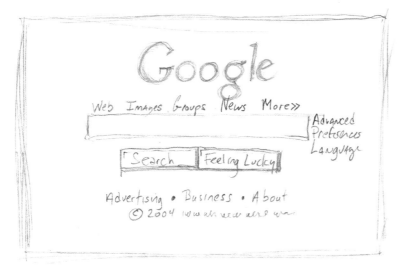

The Literal Method can also be used to conceptualize a graphic description of actions.

LITERAL METHOD

Description: Show exactly what is being described. Show the action, event, location, or object. Rather than explain it, show it.

When to Use: When something is being described. When communicating the physical characteristics and/or attributes of an action, event, location, or object apply this method.

Benefit: It is the easiest way to communicate the physical characteristics or attributes of an action, event, location, or object.

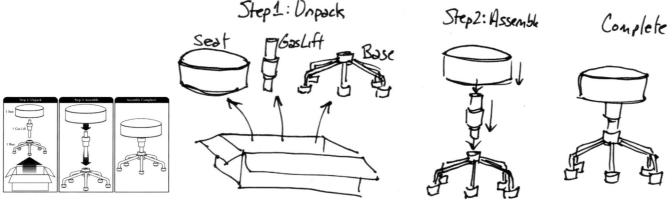

Most weight-loss sales campaigns use the familiar "before and after" graphic. They show the results you could have if you used their product or service. Seeing real people, objects, situations, events, locations, and results establishes credibility and builds trust while communicating the information.

Other examples of the Literal Method include cutaway diagrams, cross section diagrams, exploded diagrams, maps, and photographs or renderings that stay **true to reality.**

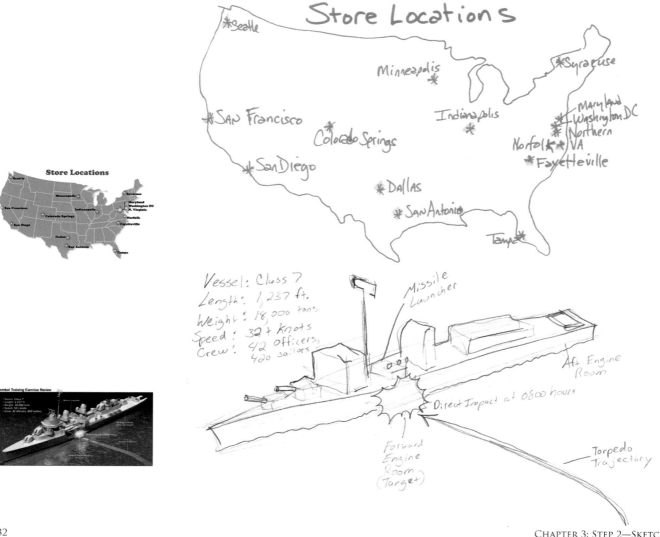

CHAPTER 3: STEP 2—SKETCH

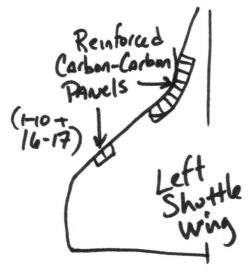

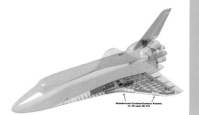

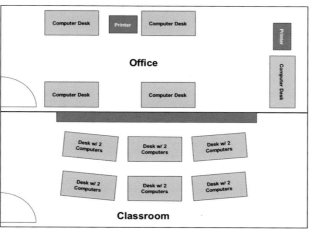

Continuing Medical Education (CME) interactive tutorials educate medical professionals on recent findings in their fields of study. CME tutorials typically supplement text and audio descriptions with a picture, video, graphic, or animation. The imagery significantly aids in the audience's understanding of the presented information.

The audience wants to see it before they buy it. Brian Tracy, a leading authority on the development of human potential and personal effectiveness, said on his CD *The Psychology of Selling,* "People … make decisions based on stories and word **pictures.**" He goes on to say, "People think in terms of pictures not in terms of statistics." In his book, *Advanced Selling Strategies,* he says, "Human beings are intensely visual. What a customer sees has **22 times** the impact of something he hears." If you are selling lawn furniture, show the lawn furniture. If you are selling home restoration services, show your before and after pictures. The same is true for most graphics. If you are selling a new idea, product or service, show it to the audience. If you are trying to get "buy in" on an innovative new gear assembly, show the new gear assembly and point out the innovations. You could even show the old gear assembly for comparison.

SUBSTITUTION METHOD

Step 1: Review Data	Step 2: Decide on Imagery	Step 3: Render or Assemble
Look for abstract concepts or concepts and entities that may be hard for the audience to understand or relate to.	Substitute one concept or entity for another. It must share similar characteristics, attributes, or have the same meaning (i.e., a symbol). Use imagery that is easy for the target audience to recognize and relate to and aids in the description or definition of the subject.	Render the image. When dealing with multiple visual substitutions, the Assembly Method helps organize your visual synonyms into a construct that tells the appropriate story.

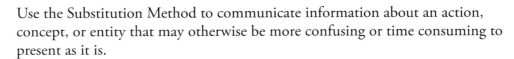

SUBSTITUTION METHOD

Description: Substitute an image of one action, concept, or entity for another. Use imagery that is easy for your target audience to recognize and relate to and aids in the description or definition of the subject.

When to Use: To communicate an abstract concept or information that may be difficult for the audience to understand and relate to use this method.

Benefit: Substituting or adding a familiar image of an action, concept, or entity increases the audience's understanding of and comfort with the subject matter. It also connects the attributes associated with the substituted imagery to your information.

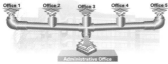

Use the Substitution Method to communicate information about an action, concept, or entity that may otherwise be more confusing or time consuming to present as it is.

You can choose from two approaches when using the Substitution Method:

1) A **visual metaphor, simile,** or **analogy** will make an implicit comparison.

2) A **symbol** will quickly communicate an action, concept, or entity.

Water flowing through a pipe can be a **visual metaphor** for the path paperwork takes in an organization because both share the same characteristics. By showing the paperwork in a pipe, the audience understands that the paperwork is flowing (moving from one point to another) through the organization along a specific path. Use the communicative and easily digested characteristics of one action, concept, or entity (water flowing through a pipe) to help clarify and/or explain another (the path paperwork takes in an organization).

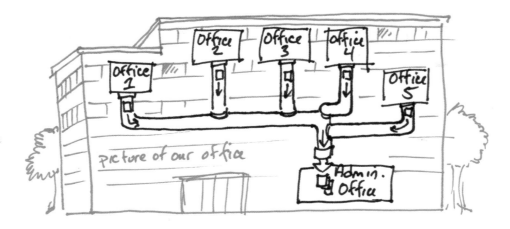

A visual metaphor operates the same as metaphors found in literature. Consider the following statement: the ship plows the sea. The ship doesn't really "plow" the sea but the metaphor creates a clear mental image that is synonymous with the message or idea the author was communicating. In addition, a visual metaphor increases the likelihood that your subject is remembered while affecting the state of mind of your target audience.

A **visual simile** is any visual that is logically relevant to an action, concept, or entity making a comparison in an effort to improve communication. For example, "achieving the end result" is like finding a pot of gold at the end of a rainbow. Therefore, a graphic of a pot of gold at the end of a rainbow helps to communicate the "achieving the end result" concept cognitively and emotionally. Like a visual metaphor, a visual simile increases the likelihood that the subject is remembered while affecting the state of mind of the target audience.

QUICK NOTE

You can also use the Substitution Method to add interest to an otherwise dry topic.

Achieving the
end result

A **visual analogy** is similar to a visual metaphor and simile. All three show similarities between actions, concepts, and entities in an effort to clarify and/or explain or push a specific agenda. Unlike visual metaphors or similes, a visual analogy is often considered a story in which a variety of attributes are compared. It is an effective tool to form logical arguments: if two different things are similar in one way, they might be similar in other ways as well. It can be used to help the audience reach a specific conclusion. For example, the author of the next graphic wants the audience to conclude that the new office is better.

Old Office

New Office

Almost all concepts contain elements that can be filtered down into basic visual metaphors, similes, or analogies. Recognizable imagery aids in the definition of the subject. Always choose recognizable imagery that is relevant to or best describes the action, concept, or entity. Use your insight into your target audience to guarantee clear communication.

In the next example, I created a graphic to support the textual headline, "Healthcare Favors the Rich." I used a **symbol** of a caduceus to quickly communicate the concept of health or healthcare. The image of the doctor reinforces the subject matter.

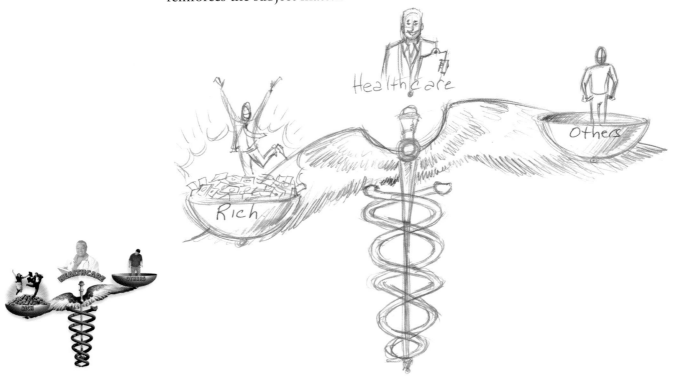

The Quantitative Method is fairly straightforward. Look for descriptions of quantity: amounts, time frames, or values that are almost always expressed numerically (even if they are estimates or notional). Then determine which type of quantitative graphic would best communicate the data.

Area charts, bar charts, bubble charts, calendars, candlestick charts, circle charts, dashboards, Gantt charts, line charts, pie charts, point charts, tables (or matrices), and timelines make up the majority of graphic types used to effectively communicate quantitative data.

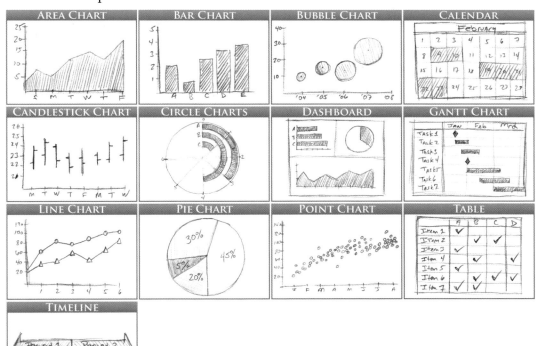

QUANTITATIVE METHOD

Description: Use a quantitative graphic to quickly communicate, analyze, and compare amounts, time frames, and values. Quantitative graphics include area charts, bar charts, bubble charts, calendars, candlestick charts, circle charts, dashboards, Gantt charts, line charts, pie charts, point charts, tables, and timelines.

When to Use: When you are communicating amounts, time frames, and values apply this method.

Benefit: Presenting data graphically helps your audience quickly digest the information. A viewer, without much effort or understanding of the data, can locate and analyze trends and quickly find similar, larger, or smaller values. A quantitative graphic organizes data for quick and memorable analysis.

Avoid a data dump. Make your numbers interesting and easy to remember. Use the right graphic and link the data to a benefit. Show your audience why your numbers matter to them.

Keep in mind that area, bar, circle, line, pie, and point charts can display the same data. However, some are better suited for communicating your messages—it depends on the primary objective of the graphic. Choosing the best graphic type can mean the difference between success and failure, since each graphic type presents and "spins" the data differently. For example, if your goal is to emphasize a vastly disparate dollar amount paid for onsite security services versus other security services, you may find a pie chart is a better choice than a bar chart because the pie chart more effectively communicates the percentages of the total amount.

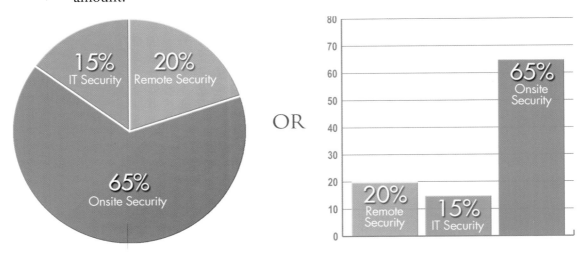

Once you choose a quantitative graphic type, you may want to emphasize or de-emphasize the data. Overstating or understating the data using scale affects your target audience's *perception* of the presented data without changing the amounts, time frames, or values.

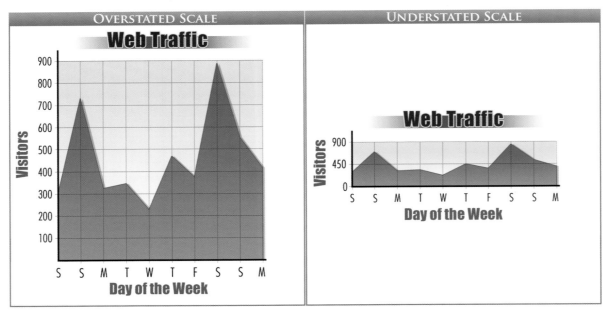

In the overstated graphic, the number of visitors seems greater than the same numbers shown in the understated graphic. Although the data presented in both graphics is accurate, the perception of the magnitude has changed. I am sharing this graphic to demonstrate how scale can affect the audience's perception of the information. I do *not* advocate the use of scale to exaggerate claims or intentionally mislead audiences. Manipulative use of overstated or understated scale will result in your audience mistrusting the data and, by association, the presenter.

The following examination of each quantitative graphic type will help you choose how best to represent your data.

An **area chart** depicts continuous quantitative data usually over time using filled areas to communicate amount, time frame, or value. An area chart is traditionally used to analyze changes in amounts or values over time.

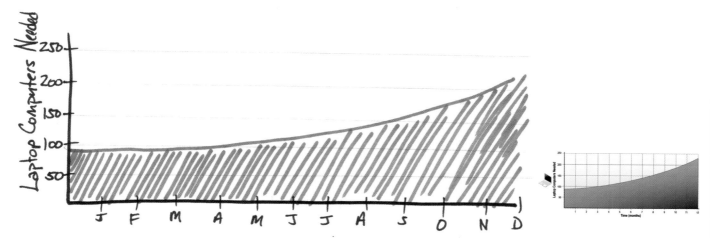

A **bar chart** depicts the changes in quantitative data using "bars," where the size of each bar represents the proportional value of the quantitative data. A bar chart is traditionally used to compare the differences between amounts, time frames, or values of actions, concepts, or entities.

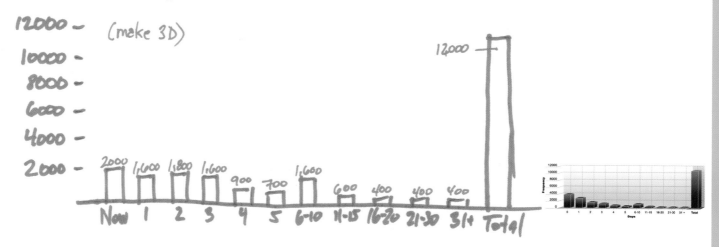

A **bubble chart** is used best for communicating a broader data range. It can also communicate the uncertainty of a predicted amount, time frame, or value. It is possible to do the same with other charts but the bubble chart is most suited for communicating concepts that depend on a data range.

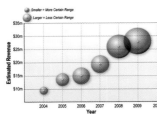

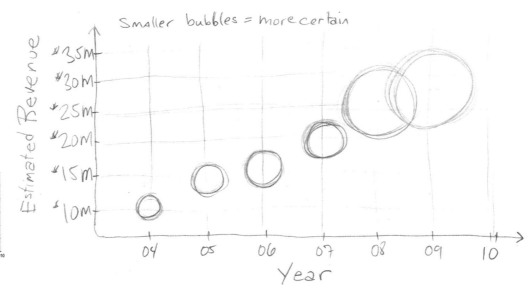

Candlestick charts are typically used to present and analyze stock, bond, and commodity (and other securities) values. Price is shown in the vertical axis and time in the horizontal axis. They can be used to present other forms of data but be aware of the association of the candlestick chart to stock values.

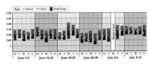

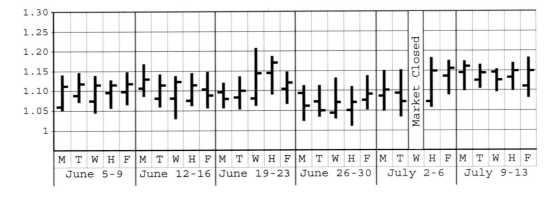

Calendars, Gantt charts, and **timelines** are very effective ways to convey schedules. A calendar is a table showing years, months, weeks, and days. A Gantt chart is essentially a bar chart representing time and activity used for planning, tracking, and controlling schedules. A timeline is a graphic that linearly represents time.

The following graphic illustrates the ability of a **Gantt chart** to communicate a complex project schedule.

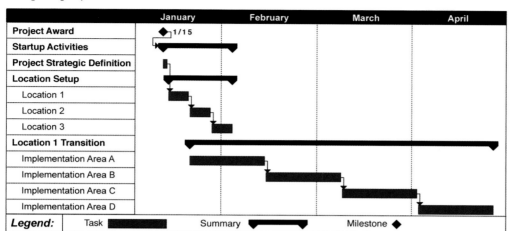

QUICK NOTE

As seen in this Gantt chart example, many quantitative graphics can be conceptualized in Microsoft Office. For example, Gantt Charts can be developed in MS Project, tables in MS Word, and most charts in MS Excel.

Timelines are less detailed but quicker to assimilate.

Circle charts are a family of graphics that display quantitative data using a circular format and includes radar graphs, sector graphs, circle column graphs, and many similarly shaped graphics. In general, I have found circle charts are not as communicative as other quantitative graphic types.

Employee Retention

QUICK NOTE

Gauge graphics are a subset of dashboard graphics. Gauge graphics can also act as visual metaphors when showing quantitative data.

A **dashboard graphic** presents multiple metrics (usually employing multiple graphic types) in one consolidated format. Think of your car's dashboard. Dashboards, if designed properly, are very effective at communicating large quantities of data.

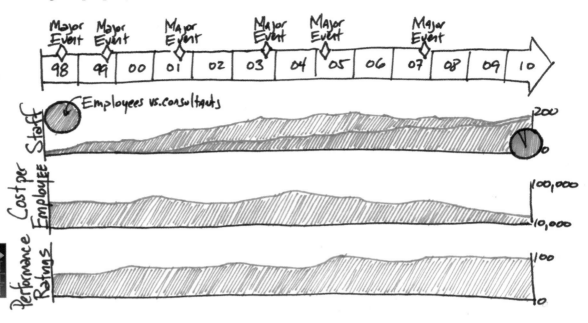

A **line chart** shows the changes in quantitative data using lines, where the position of a line represents the proportional value of the data. Line charts, like area charts, are traditionally used to analyze changes in amounts or values over time.

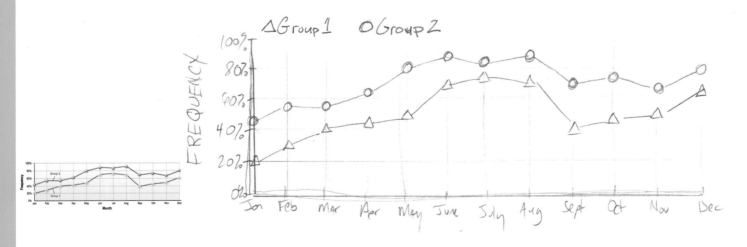

A **point chart** shows quantitative data using plotted points. (In some instances connecting the points results in a line graph.) Point charts are traditionally used to show frequency or correlations between actions, concepts, or entities.

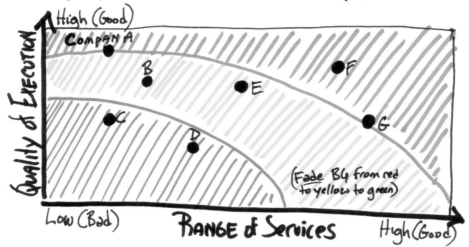

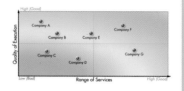

For our purposes, a **table** and **matrix** are synonymous. A table is a grid that correlates data along two axes. (Please note, not all tables communicate quantitative data.)

Clients	1	2	3	4	5	6	7	8	9	10	11	12	13	Total
# of Trainers	91	35	32	26	10	25	15	37	4	4	11	12	10	312
# of Instructors	48	20	14	14	8	5	14	34	0	4	8	3	2	174
# of Authors	25	7	6	10	3	0	2	4	0	4	4	3	0	68

Pie charts communicate percentages of the whole using proportional segments.

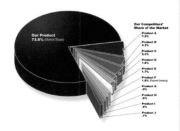

Pie charts are also known as segmented charts because they do not have to be circular. Any visual element that can be segmented to communicate proportional amounts, time frames, or values is acceptable. For example, what if you wanted to show how much your company is spending on office supplies? What image depicts spending? A credit card, check, dollar sign, or maybe a dollar bill? Choose one of those images and segment it into various colored sections proportional with the amount spent. Assign titles, amounts, and icons to label the segments to effectively communicate the data. The following graphic illustrates how you can use basic quantitative graphic principles to create a unique, communicative spin on a classic graphic type.

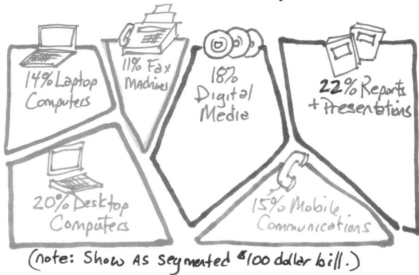

There are often many ways to show the same information. I have seen combinations of several graphic types. It is not always necessary for quantitative data to be illustrated by the graphic types previously listed in this method. The following example combines a basic process diagram and a timeline.

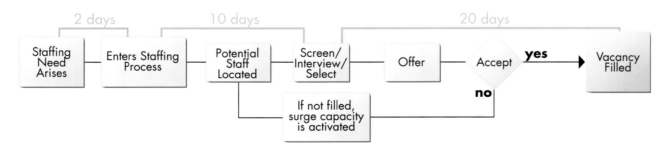

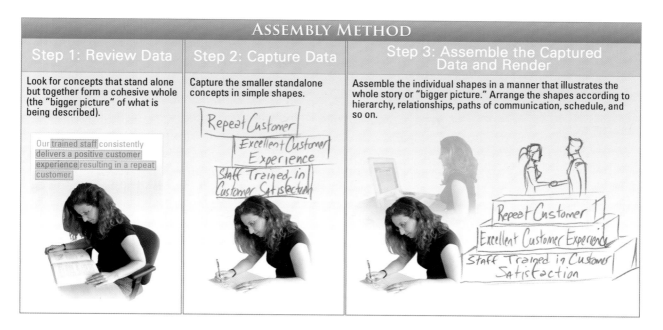

ASSEMBLY METHOD

Step 1: Review Data

Look for concepts that stand alone but together form a cohesive whole (the "bigger picture" of what is being described).

Our trained staff consistently delivers a positive customer experience resulting in a repeat customer.

Step 2: Capture Data

Capture the smaller standalone concepts in simple shapes.

Repeat Customer

Excellent Customer Experience

Staff Trained in Customer Satisfaction

Step 3: Assemble the Captured Data and Render

Assemble the individual shapes in a manner that illustrates the whole story or "bigger picture." Arrange the shapes according to hierarchy, relationships, paths of communication, schedule, and so on.

Repeat Customer

Excellent Customer Experience

Staff Trained in Customer Satisfaction

Imagine children's building blocks—your goal is to assemble an image that uses graphical hierarchy and other design techniques to depict an action, concept, or entity. Each unique element of the topic to be clarified and/or explained becomes a basic shape (a building block). Basic shapes help organize your data into digestible chunks that are pieced together to tell the whole story.

When using written documentation to conceptualize, read a section of text and "capture" standalone elements. Then place those pieces of text into a basic shape such as a square. Continue to do this until the entire concept is broken down into standalone chunks and captured in squares or blocks. Use this method to create a graphic for the following text:

> BOGL has a four-phase process for introducing new technology. Phase One involves training and mentoring. Phase Two is the final removal of the old tools and the introduction of the new computers. Phase Three provides onsite IT support 24x7 for one month. Phase Four submits, collects, and takes action using a formal evaluation.

Phase One of a four-phase plan becomes one of four blocks. Phase Two of a four-phase plan becomes the second of four blocks. And so on …

Now assemble the blocks into a structure that is synonymous with the relationships discovered in your research. To determine positioning ask yourself questions like the following: What element is the foundation? What element supports the next? What is the end result?

You are using the blocks to assemble a visual representation of the information (the big picture). Your goal is to assemble the blocks in a way that shows the hierarchy, relationships, paths of communication, actions, and any other needs.

ASSEMBLY METHOD

Description: As you review the data to be visually depicted, capture standalone textual elements (ideas, concepts, benefits, goals, departments, systems, etc.) in boxes. Assemble these boxes in a manner that illustrates the "big picture." Arrange the boxes according to hierarchy, relationships, paths of communication, actions, and so on (also known as "chunking").

When to Use: When starting a graphic or when there is a lot of content.

Benefit: It helps you identify the most salient and relevant content. Basic building principles make it easy to quickly create a "big picture" view of the information. The audience can see how each piece supports the whole process. It also decreases visual clutter and confusion.

The final image should illustrate how the blocks come together to form a cohesive whole.

If the blocks contain steps in a linear process arrange them so the steps are in their appropriate order of occurrence.

  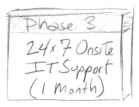 

This process is also known as "chunking." You are breaking content into bite-sized chunks that can then be reassembled to show an overview of the content presented.

You can substitute basic shapes with objects that support your graphic's messages. Try using a visual metaphor, simile, or analogy (Substitution Method) that supports either the message to be communicated or the overall action, concept, or entity depicted. What type of imagery could enhance the telling of your story? Perhaps arrows represent each phase or the phases could be "steps" that lead to the ultimate goal or future state. In the next image, I modified my shapes to look like steps on a building. After further information gathering, I find that there are departments within BOGL that the four phases support and in turn these departments support the future of BOGL.

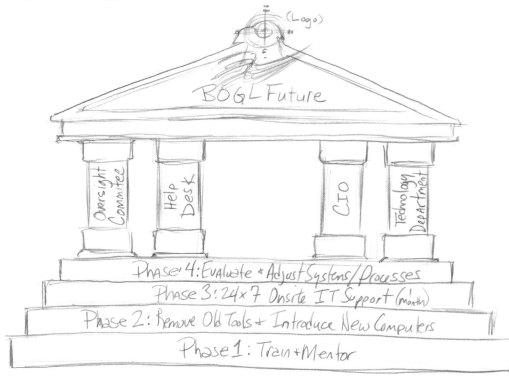

The imagery you select comes with preexisting meanings and associations; therefore, choose your visual elements carefully. In the previous visual, the temple graphic may convey permanence, stability, structure, and longevity. If these descriptors are supportive of, or part of, your graphic's intended messages, then it is successful. However, depending on the target audience and subject matter, the temple graphic may communicate that the proposed solution is antiquated or outdated. Your understanding of your subject matter and your target audience will determine what imagery best communicates the messages needed for your graphic to be successful.

The following are examples of graphics that were developed using the Assembly Method.

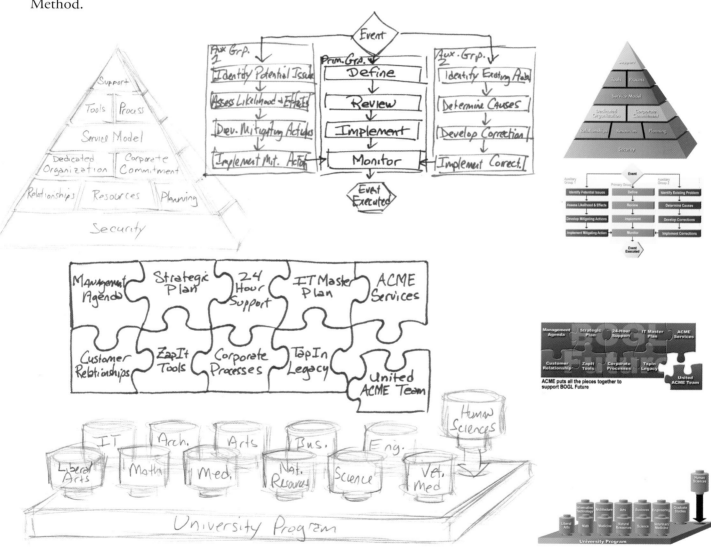

QUICK NOTE

Are you stuck? For new, effective ways of showing your ideas, turn to *Chapter 6: Graphic Types* on page 85.

Another option is to visit BizGraphicsOnDemand.com or go to Google and choose the image search option to see what subject-specific imagery others have used.

For most conceptualization projects, begin with the Assembly Method. It is the fastest, most effective way to process large quantities of information and create a graphic skeleton. From this point you can move to another method, or use multiple methods, to further evolve the graphic into a communicative visual. Use whatever method is needed to best improve communication.

You can use multiple approaches in any given image but do not overcomplicate your graphic with too many visual elements. The resulting graphic may be difficult for your audience to quickly and accurately digest. Too many graphical elements cause confusion, add visual noise, and greatly interfere with communication.

DESIGN TECHNIQUES

When conceptualizing successful graphics you will often repeatedly express the same concepts. The following are frequently encountered concepts and effective ways to illustrate them. Use these design techniques to increase your graphic's ability to communicate the right information the right way.

This is not a comprehensive list. Only those design techniques that are used often and effectively for the widest spectrum of audiences are included. Your experience will yield new conceptual needs and different design techniques for graphically communicating the concepts. Remember, each audience is unique. Before choosing a design technique be sure the visual elements communicate that which is intended to your target audience.

- **Connectivity or Flow/Direction**—Lines indicate connectivity and arrows indicate connectivity and flow/direction.

- **Supplemental, Infrequent, or Less Influential Relationships**—Use transparency or muted colors and dashed lines to indicate a visual element occurs infrequently, is supplemental, or is less influential than other elements.

- **Future/Past State**—A timeline and transparency or muted colors and dashed lines are effective techniques to indicate an element is "to be" or "once was."

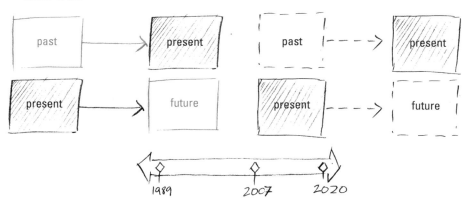

 QUICK NOTE

Roads, paths, and arrows fading into the distance are also accepted ways to illustrate a future or past state.

- **Cooperation and Synthesis**—A convergence of graphic elements communicates synthesis and alludes to the cooperation that must occur to achieve that synthesis.

- **Interaction and Influence**—Visually connecting graphic elements in any way indicates interaction and alludes to the influence and cooperation that must occur between the separate elements.

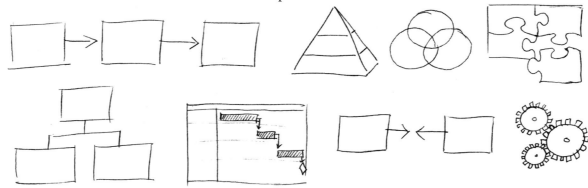

 QUICK NOTE

For complex explanations, link detailed graphics to an icon of an established overview graphic with a blowout.

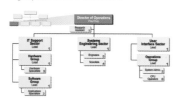

- **Details or Descriptions**—Blowouts and callouts are great for providing additional details or descriptions to visual elements within your graphics.

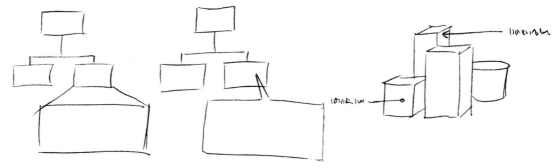

50

- **Grouping**—There are three ways to group: using a similar physical appearance, organized positioning, and constraining or linking lines or shapes.

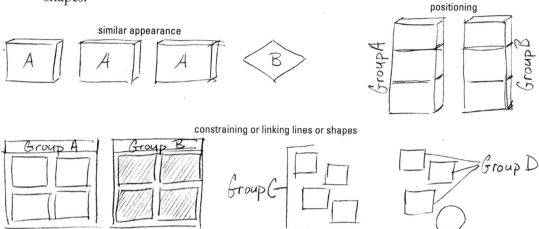

- **Hierarchy**—Use color, shade, and positioning to illustrate hierarchy.

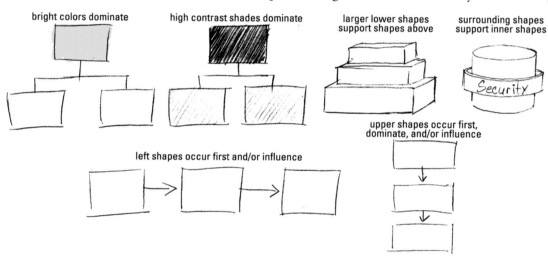

QUICK NOTE

Visual hierarchy can also be used to subtly control where the audience focuses their attention.

Keep in mind that aesthetic hierarchy and highlighting are achieved through the relativity of surrounding elements. In order for something to have visual dominance, other graphic elements must graphically recede. Too many visually dominant graphic elements diminish the effect and often result in an unsuccessful graphic.

- **Highlighting**—Contrasting colors, shades, sizes, and visual complexity work best at drawing attention.

cooperation teamwork process manufacturing

security   security   security   security

- **Icons and Symbols**—An icon is defined as a representational graphic element that is visually analogous with an action, concept, or entity. A symbol is a representational graphic element that has a *learned* meaning or accepted connotation for an action, concept, or entity.

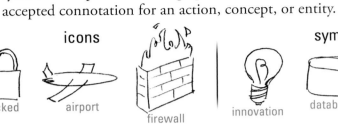

- **Organization**—There are five ways to organize information: alphabetical/sequential, time, magnitude, category, and location.

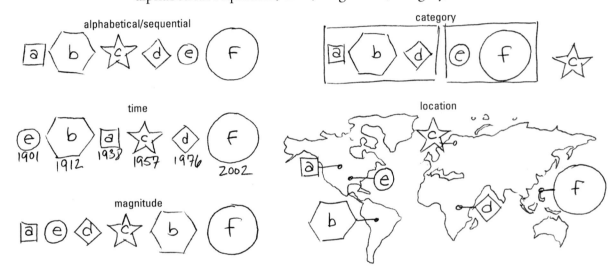

- **Order vs. Disorder**—Horizontal and vertical lines or arrows, alignment, and equal spacing between visual elements convey a sense of order and control. Diagonal lines or arrows, misalignment, and unequal spacing between objects convey a sense of disorder and a lack of control. Unnecessary intersecting/overlapping graphic elements also indicate to the audience that what is shown is disorganized and unmanageable.

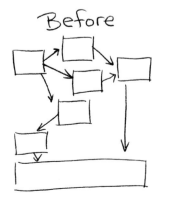
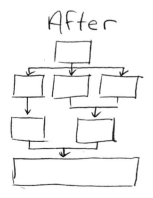

• **Space Constraints**—Use a continuation arrow, scale break, or page break to indicate that some information was omitted due to page constraints.

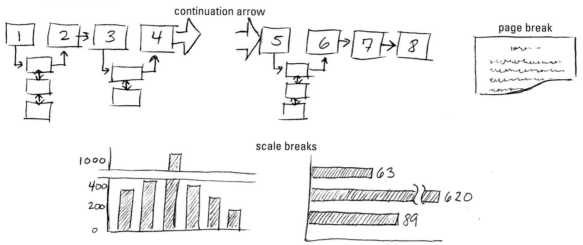

continuation arrow

page break

scale breaks

QUICK NOTE

According to Dale Carnegie
Training, the presenter is
judged by what the audience
sees. Make sure that the
image portrayed by your
visuals elicits the appropriate
reaction.

 QUICK NOTE

The strategies for affecting
emotions communicate the
importance or urgency of a
charitable cause.

 QUICK NOTE

According to neurologist and
Nobel Laureate Eric Kandel,
it is easier to repress
cognitive experiences than
it is to repress emotional
experiences.

(Susan Kruglinski, "Does
Psychotherapy Work," *Discover*
[April 2006]: 58-61)

AFFECTING EMOTIONS

This section shares strategies for influencing, motivating, and emotionally affecting your audience. If your goal is to communicate data **and** influence your audience, you can include additional visual elements intended to affect emotions. Your data must remain factual, but you can add other visual cues that help guide your audience to an intended conclusion. I do not recommend or condone sensationalism, scare tactics, or any action that might be seen as an unethical business practice. Instead, the strategies for affecting emotions are intended to increase the likelihood that your graphic will receive the attention it needs to be absorbed, understood, remembered, and achieve its primary objective.

Edward Tufte, Professor Emeritus at Yale University and author of many information design books, believes that information graphics, in their purest form, should exclude all unnecessary aesthetic elements (colors, drop shadows, beveled edges, photographs, etc.) that may cloud the audience's interpretation of the presented data. He is right. Visual information that has no relevance to the communication of the data is a detriment to the purpose—objective communication of data for analysis—of an information graphic. Many disciplines such as academics, mathematics, journalism, and the sciences depend on "no spin" empirical data to objectively reach conclusions and find solutions. Objective statistical analysis could be corrupted by unnecessary aesthetic information.

However, most graphics are expected to do more than just present data for dissemination. As stated earlier, in the world of visual communication there are two principal needs: communicate information and influence or motivate the audience.

Aside from fine art and those graphics used for pure statistical analysis of empirical data, almost all graphics are persuading an audience to agree with the presenter and arrive at an intended conclusion. *Time* and *Discover* magazines use compelling topics and beautifully rendered graphics to better communicate the presented information and data **and** help convey their competency and professionalism, hold the audience's attention, help establish their credibility and dominance as premiere news sources, and sell more magazines. Periodicals compete with other forms of media. Television, for example, uses emotionally charged content, flashy graphics, colors, sounds, music, and attractive people to help maintain or expand its audience. Mainstream media of every type must maintain or grow their viewership to survive by employing stimulating, compelling topics and visuals that grab and hold the audience's attention long enough to be digested so they will accomplish their goals.

Imagine receiving an issue of *Time* that only presented the facts without aesthetic embellishment or concern for emotional appeal? What would happen to their distribution?

Everything about their magazine is consistent with their agenda. The same must be true for your graphics. It is not sufficient for visuals to simply communicate data when an agenda is present—and there is almost always an agenda.

STRATEGIES TO AFFECT EMOTIONS THROUGH CONTENT

Maslow's Hierarchy of Needs

An extremely effective technique to affecting emotions is to use *Maslow's Hierarchy of Needs*. Abraham Maslow, a well-respected physiologist, developed the widely accepted theory of a hierarchy of needs. He postulated that human beings are motivated by unsatisfied needs and basic needs must be met before higher needs can be satisfied.

The needs, in order of importance, are as follows:

1) **Safety and Survival**—Breathing, food, and water are the most important and trump all other needs.

2) **Security**—Physical, financial, and emotional security defeat lower needs.

3) **Love and Belonging**—We need to feel accepted by others and belong to a larger social group.

4) **Esteem**—We need to feel liked and respected in order to like and respect ourselves.

5) **Self-actualization**—We need to believe we are becoming all that we can become.

6) **Truth**—We search for truth through the study of philosophy and religion.

7) **Beauty**—We appreciate music, art, dance—that which is beautiful.

Maslow believed the more basic the need, the more powerful the appeal. You can use this information to help influence your target audience. If your graphic taps into an emotion associated with a baser need than your competition, you win. For example, if a graphic talks of beauty and another appeals to a sense of survival, the latter will be more effective than the former. Which ad is more compelling?

This skin cancer warning depends upon the audience's vanity to motivate.

This skin cancer warning depends upon the audience's survival instinct to motivate.

The graphic's subject matter dictates how basic the need can be. If possible, be creative. A little forethought and a new approach will get you that much closer to a baser need.

Fear and Greed

Another effective technique is to appeal to your audience's fear and greed. There are two major motivators: the desire for gain and the fear of loss. According to physiologists, the fear of loss is 2.5 times greater than the desire for gain. Keep this fact in mind when developing your messages. For example, a graphic communicating the need to save your money in a bank is more persuasive when it shows a burglar taking money from your home rather than showing you earning interest by banking.

Greed, however, is not to be ignored. How compelling are signs for FREE stuff? Using the audience's desire for greater compensation, a bigger house, or a new car is a proven technique to motivate people to take action.

Familiarity

Familiarity elicits feelings of comfort and trust. Showing your audience the people, places, or things they know and like can be powerfully persuasive. We feel comfortable when surrounded by recognizable, familiar things. We feel uneasy and are often on guard when introduced to unfamiliar things. We scrutinize the new thing and accept the familiar. For example, you would choose a trusted, respected friend's advice over a stranger's. You would probably choose a familiar auto mechanic over one you have never used. You trust the known more than the unknown. Elicit that comfort level/trust from your target audience by using familiar elements to communicate that your solution is lower risk. Imagine hiring a company to run your marketing firm. Two companies compete for your business, Company Alpha and Company Beta. During their presentation, Company Alpha shows their organizational chart with names and positions. However, Company Beta presents their organizational chart with photographs of their management staff. Immediately, you recognize two of the employees as friends from your college. Who are you more comfortable hiring?

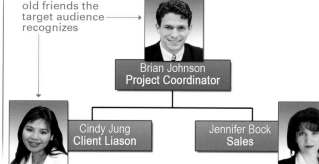

When I am creating a graphic for a client who has a relationship with their target audience I show a picture of my client, if appropriate, and any other imagery

 **QUICK NOTE**

If you doubt that fear is a greater motivator than greed, ask a friend these two questions: "Will you harm another person if I paid you $1,000? Would you harm a person who tried to take your $1,000?"

QUICK NOTE

It is subconsciously comforting to hear a familiar voice as opposed to a "stranger's" voice. This is why corporations use high-priced celebrities to do the voiceovers for their television commercials.

When applicable, use familiarity to help your audience feel that the solution you are presenting is lower risk.

with which the audience is familiar and partial (e.g., the audience's offices, colleagues, products, marketing materials, or website).

Positive Images

Show your audience imagery that makes them feel good. Show pretty places and things. Show happy, appropriately attractive people who epitomize what you expect the user of the service or product to look like enjoying the benefits of what is presented. Your audience, if interested, will imagine themselves—or others they know—enjoying "it" as well. Their emotions will be involved in their evaluation to a greater degree.

Pay attention to any advertising that you see on television and in magazines. Look for advertisements that show happy, attractive people receiving the benefit of using the product or engaging in the service. Those ads are using your emotions to reach their primary objective. Neurologists found that when we see attractive people the same part of our brain that is stimulated with cocaine use is activated and makes feel good. We are programmed to feel compassion when we see babies. How does seeing a puppy or kitten make you feel?

The following dashboard graphic about baby facts and statistics uses an image of an infant to not only communicate the subject matter but also influence the mood of the reader.

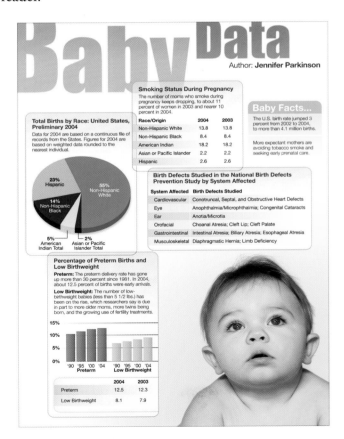

The purpose of showing positive imagery is to stimulate the reward centers in the brains of your audience, which will then be associated with the presented material. The likelihood that your visual will achieve its primary objective is far higher.

Negative Images

Show disturbing images to emphasize the importance of an applicable subject. *When appropriate*, shock your audience to get their attention or show images that motivate the audience to be proactive. The following example uses an unsettling visual to motivate the audience to take action.

QUICK NOTE

In addition to subject matter, framing, angle, and lighting drastically change the mood of a photograph. Make sure that your picture evokes the right feelings in your audience. When in doubt, ask for a second opinion.

The purpose of showing negative imagery is to stimulate the pain centers in the brains of your audience, which will then be associated with the presented material. The thought of ignoring such atrocities might be too much to bear. (Beware: When you expose your audience to any negative emotion, you run the risk of pushing them away.)

STRATEGIES TO AFFECT EMOTIONS THROUGH AESTHETICS

QUICK NOTE

Studies have shown that manipulating visual design factors could induce a target emotion such as trustworthiness.

(J. Kim and J.Y. Moon, "Designing Towards Emotional Usability in Customer Interfaces—Trustworthiness of Cyber-banking System Interfaces," *Interacting with Computers* Volume 10: Issue 1 [March 1998]: 1-29)

Aesthetically Appealing

Aesthetically appealing graphics elicit positive emotions. For example, beautiful works of art evoke specific emotions in its viewers that can transcend generations. We are drawn to beauty. The more attractive your visual, the longer it will be studied and admired. People are hardwired to like, feel good about, be drawn to, and be influenced by attractive graphics. Visually appealing, audience-focused, error-free, clear and concise graphics usually achieve their primary objectives. A graphic that is professionally rendered by a designer with formal training in visual art has a higher chance of success than a graphic rendered by non-designers who do not follow the principles in this book.

Which of the following two graphics is more appealing and, therefore, more likely to have greater influence? Describe the company that presents graphic Ⓐ? Describe the company that presents graphic Ⓑ?

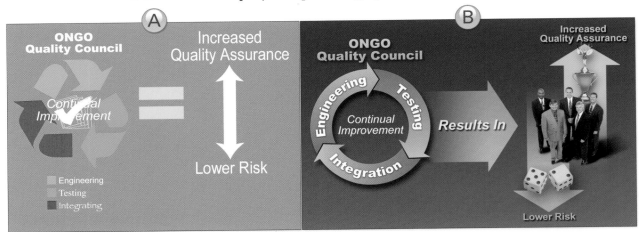

Color

QUICK NOTE

- Color increases the willingness of the audience to read by 80%.

- Color improves comprehension up to 75%.

- Color increases recognition up to 78%.

- Color increases motivation and participation up to 80%.

Color is extremely effective at influencing the mood of the viewer. In the next graphic, the color affects the pie's appeal. Both colors evoke very different responses. Which piece of pie would you eat?

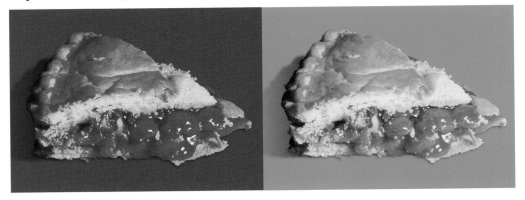

In her book, *Visual Literacy: Learn to See, See to Learn*, Dr. Lynell Burmark says that 80% of a person's impression of a product is based on its color and that using color enhances learning and improves retention by more than 75%. She says colors evoke specific predictable responses. Although true, keep in mind, those predictable responses presuppose that colors are chosen by someone with a good understanding of the target audience's interpretation of color. Color can have different connotations based on subject matter and culture. The following is a list of colors and their possible corresponding emotional responses (specific to many Western cultures):

- Red = empowering, bold (If used in large quantities, studies show that red can have a physical effect, increasing the rate of respiration and raising blood pressure. This can negatively affect mood.)

- Orange = warmth, happiness

- Yellow = happiness, energy (excellent for highlighting)

- Green = balance, refreshing (usually makes a good secondary color)

- Blue = relaxing, cool (usually the safest/most appealing color to use for business graphic color schemes)

- Violet = comforting

- White = pure, associated with cleanliness

- Black = authoritative, shows discipline

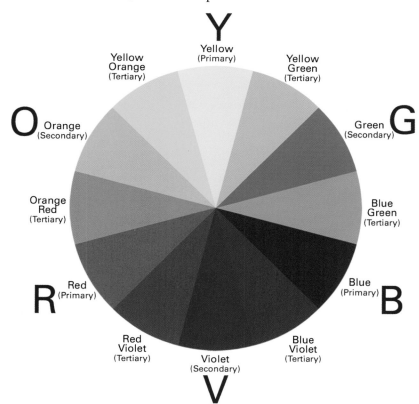

QUICK NOTE

Color consists of three variables:

- Hue – where on the color wheel the color appears

- Saturation – the intensity or vibrancy of the color

- Value – the lightness or darkness of the color

QUICK NOTE

There are two key "groupings" of colors:

- Analogous – colors that appear next to one another on the color wheel like blue, green, and yellow

- Complementary – colors that are across from one another on the color wheel like red and green

Analogous colors are often the better choice when developing your color palette because complementary colors vibrate when next to one another.

QUICK NOTE

Use the acronym ROY G. BiV to remember the color positions on the color wheel.

R = Red

O = Orange

Y = Yellow

G = Green

B = Blue

i = indigo (not a primary color)

V = Violet

Colors have preexisting, subject-specific, and culturally dependent meanings. Red in many Western cultures can be associated with both love and danger. In the following example, red is associated with a negative concept (risk) whereas green is associated with a positive concept (safety).

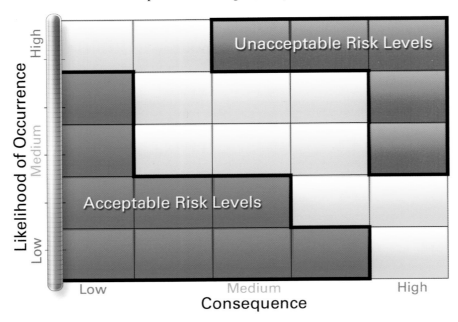

In other cultures, red is associated with completely different emotions and ideas. In China, for example, red is the color of happiness and prosperity. In India and Pakistan, red is worn by brides. In South Africa, it is the color of mourning. Before choosing a color, know your audience. Research how the audience will interpret your aesthetic choices.

Learn as much as you can about your target audience prior to choosing your color palette to ensure the clearest communication and predictable emotional responses.

Shapes and Lines

Shapes and lines, to a lesser extent than color, also affect the mood of the viewer. Diagonal shapes and lines are more dynamic and energetic. However, used in excess, the resulting mood is usually negative, evoking feelings of uneasiness or agitation. Too many diagonals, for example, result in a graphic that appears disorganized and disheveled. The graphic is usually difficult to follow. Horizontal and vertical shapes and lines provide a sense of stability. Using a horizontal and vertical layout communicates that the presented information is organized and controlled. Curved shapes and lines (circles, ovals, etc.) are soothing and calming and can help pacify your target audience. Curved, horizontal, and vertical shapes and lines often result in a positive mood.

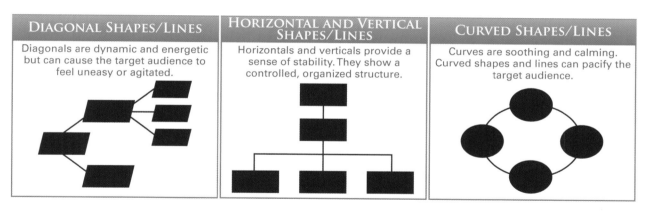

DIAGONAL SHAPES/LINES	HORIZONTAL AND VERTICAL SHAPES/LINES	CURVED SHAPES/LINES
Diagonals are dynamic and energetic but can cause the target audience to feel uneasy or agitated.	Horizontals and verticals provide a sense of stability. They show a controlled, organized structure.	Curves are soothing and calming. Curved shapes and lines can pacify the target audience.

Choose shapes and lines that are congruent with the message you wish to communicate and the emotional state you intend to elicit. Certain shapes have predefined meanings based on subject matter and culture. Do your homework before choosing identifiable shapes.

Visual Noise

Using too many visual elements or "busy" textures/imagery causes visual noise. Visual noise often induces a negative opinion of the subject matter. The following are some examples of graphics with too much visual noise.

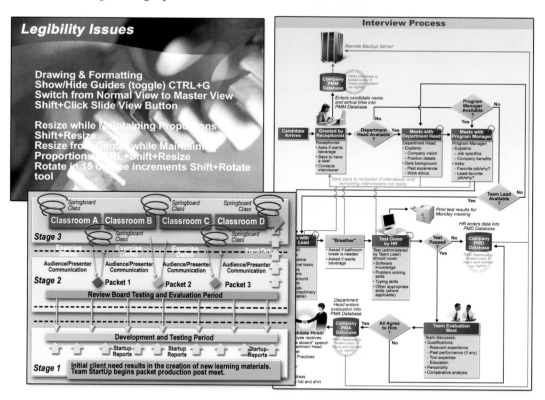

Too much visual noise results in a hard-to-follow, difficult-to-read graphic. The overall effect is usually a negative opinion of the subject matter or presenter.

However, you can use visual noise to your advantage, if your intent is to sway your target audience's opinion from that which is unwanted or unfavorable to a new proposed action, concept, or entity. To use this technique, create a graphic depicting two elements: old and new. Show the old element with lots of visual noise. Show the new element clutter free, organized, and easy to read. The audience will be drawn to the cleaner, more digestible portion of your graphic.

When creating a comparative graphic, the unwanted or unfavorable portion of the graphic should not be overtly cluttered or your intent will be too obvious. Your audience will feel manipulated, which will negatively affect their trust of the presenter. Not only will the graphic be unsuccessful, but the resulting audience state of mind could decimate all possibilities of ever achieving the presenter's goals.

Balance and Symmetry

Balance and symmetry are two additional design techniques at your disposal. Balanced graphics convey a sense of stability and support a positive state of mind. Unbalanced graphics result in a feeling of uneasiness. Aesthetic balance is achieved when the graphic's left and right sides and, to a lesser extent, top and bottom visually "weigh" similar amounts giving a sense of equilibrium. In a balanced graphic, the elements are arranged so that neither side dominates the other. Unbalanced graphics feel as if they are unstable—like they will tip to one side. The graphic elements seem unevenly distributed as shown in the next example.

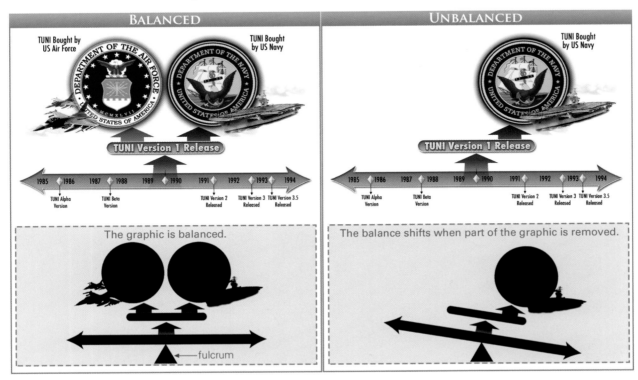

Symmetry is not necessary to achieve balance. Asymmetrical balance is more frequently found in many fine art pieces and is often used successfully by experienced artists and graphic designers.

Your audience is only mildly affected by visual balance but unbalanced graphics have a more pronounced negative effect. It is very challenging to completely balance your graphics. Do not be overly concerned—clarification and/or explanation are paramount. Achieving aesthetic balance becomes a bonus. However, always be aware of egregious balance issues: if the graphic's balance negatively affects you, it will negatively affect your target audience.

Aesthetically symmetrical graphics convey a sense order and stability. True symmetry is achieved if the graphic is equally split and both halves match.

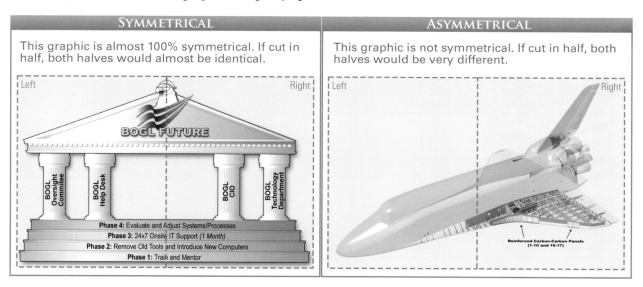

More than balance, perfect symmetry is often too challenging a goal. Additionally, an overly symmetrical layout can result in an uninspiring, boring design. If your goal is to create a dynamic graphic that captures and holds the audience's attention, then symmetry may be too visually predictable and less appealing.

Use your knowledge of the effect balance and symmetry has on your audience only when possible and appropriate. Never allow balance and symmetry to be your main tool in influencing audience mood.

Font

Font choice helps determine the mood of your graphic. Fonts range from clean and simple to gritty and intricate. The following are examples of different fonts. Notice the association you instantly make with each and the mood it elicits.

Brush Script	Chalkboard
Cooper	*Curlz*
Giddyup	Goudy Old Style
Helvetica	HERCULANUM
Impact	𝕷𝖚𝖈𝖎𝖉𝖆 𝕭𝖑𝖆𝖈𝖐𝖑𝖊𝖙𝖙𝖊𝖗
MESQUITE	ROSEWOOD
STENCIL	Zapfino

What did MESQUITE remind you of? How did it make you feel?

Choose a font that is legible (hard to read fonts will frustrate your audience) and is consistent with your content and the mood you wish to elicit. For example, if your graphic is meant to be serious and inspire trust, do not use a whimsical font like Curlz. Instead try a visually clean font such as **Helvetica**. Like any visual element, fonts have preexisting, subject-specific, and culturally dependent associations. Choose your fonts wisely.

Consistency

Stay consistent! Independent research verified that internal consistency cultivates a feeling of trust because it indicates to the audience that the information presented was designed—it was the product of careful consideration. Each visual element you choose should be intended to work with all other elements to elicit a specific response. If you mix visual signals, you risk sending mixed messages.

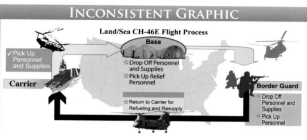

Imagine receiving a manual for your new car and each graphic is a different color and rendering style with each using different fonts. What would your opinion be of the manual's quality? What would your opinion be of the car manufacturer for providing a manual of this quality? Unfortunately, visual inconsistency is pervasive in the business environment and is one of the most odious and repeated offenses in poor graphic design.

Involving your audience's emotions is key to achieving the primary objective of your graphic because all decisions involve our emotions. Remember, everything we see elicits a specific emotional response. Know what visual element elicits what response in your target audience and you will be more successful.

QUICK NOTE

"'Design is one of the few tools that for every [dollar] you spend, you actually say something about your business … You have it in your power to use design to further the wealth and prosperity of your business.'—Raymond Turner, BAA/British Airports Authority"

(Tom Peters, *Design* [DK Publishing, Inc., 2005])

CONCEPTUALIZATION CONCLUSION

Multiple methods and techniques can be used to conceptualize one graphic. The following is an example of multiple methods and techniques woven together to make one graphic.

Let's analyze the following graphic.

Design Techniques
Color differentiates office supply categories.

Affecting Emotions
Overall mood is light and positive due to the color palette.

Four Methods
This graphic uses a combination of the following:

- **Method 1: Literal**—The images are literal depictions of each supply category.
- **Method 2: Substitution**—The standard pie chart is replaced with a segmented visual representation of money to communicate that the displayed percentages are monetary.
- **Method 3: Quantitative**—A pie chart shows the amounts spent on the different office supply categories.

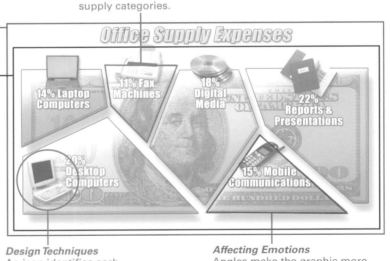

Design Techniques
An icon identifies each supply category.

Affecting Emotions
Angles make the graphic more dynamic.

As you review this book, try to identify those graphics that use multiple methods and techniques.

CHAPTER 4:
STEP 3—RENDER

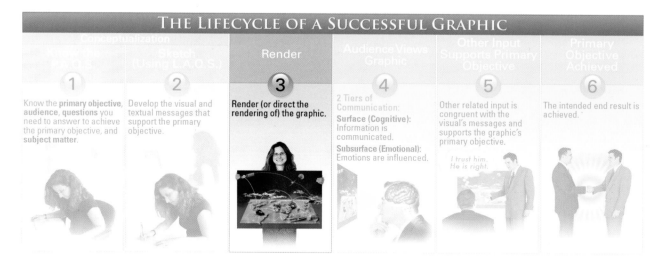

THE LIFECYCLE OF A SUCCESSFUL GRAPHIC

1 — Conceptualization (Using P.A.Q.S.) — Know the **primary objective**, **audience**, **questions** you need to answer to achieve the primary objective, and **subject matter**.

2 — Sketch (Using L.A.Q.S.) — Develop the visual and textual messages that support the primary objective.

3 — Render — Render (or direct the rendering of) the graphic.

4 — Audience Views Graphic — 2 Tiers of Communication: **Surface (Cognitive):** Information is communicated. **Subsurface (Emotional):** Emotions are influenced.

5 — Other Input Supports Primary Objective — Other related input is congruent with the visual's messages and supports the graphic's primary objective. *I trust him. He is right.*

6 — Primary Objective Achieved — The intended end result is achieved. '

Many busy business professionals are forced to render their own graphics without the support of a trained and experienced graphic designer. If you lack the time, skill, or resources to render your graphics professionally, there are solutions and strategies at your disposal.

Here are six strategies to ensure you complete your final design quickly and easily. (If you are a designer, use these strategies to get your graphics right the first time.)

1. KEEP YOUR GRAPHICS CLEAN AND SIMPLE

You may not be a superstar designer but clean, simple graphics can make you look like a professional. Non-designers often fall prey to the "more is better" syndrome. Reviewing the graphics they made, they think this doesn't "pop" or that doesn't look "good enough." That's okay. Great visual communicators know when and why to add visually appealing accents. They also know their limitations, and you should know your own. Poor visual communicators unnecessarily add distracting gradients and colors, intersecting and angled lines, bevels, shadows, text effects, 3D effects, clip art, and other over-the-top embellishments in the hope that their graphic will look better. Trust me, they are wrong. More often, the graphic looks too busy, confusing, and not professional.

Knowing the P.A.Q.S. and conceptualizing the right visual for your target audience is more important than making the most aesthetically appealing graphic. Obviously, it is an advantage to have a professionally rendered visual but sometimes that is not an option. Instead, focus on your graphic's ability to communicate the benefits of your idea, product, or service. Do this and you have a distinct advantage.

QUICK NOTE

For professional graphics and photographs go to

- BizGraphicsOnDemand.com
- iStockPhoto.com
- Dreamstime.com
- BigStockPhoto.com
- StockXpert.com
- GettyImages.com

Another option is to visit government-owned websites like Army.mil. Verify that the image you download is cleared for release and is considered public domain. This information is usually posted on the same page as their image library or on their "Privacy" or "Security" pages. Be sure to give attribution.

Keep your graphics clean and simple. This is a proven strategy to make winning business graphics, especially for professionals without formal design training. Many graphic gurus extol the virtues of simplicity in design. There are millions of success stories about professionals employing simple yet effective visuals to communicate even the most complex ideas. Use the tools you know. I recommend Microsoft PowerPoint to make your graphics. It is easy to learn, almost everyone uses it, and your graphics can be modified by anyone that uses this ubiquitous software.

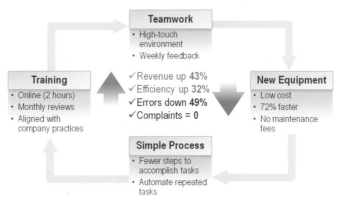

You can make simplified versions of the graphics found in Chapter 6. The goal is to use a concept that supports your graphic's primary objective. The audience-focused information communicated by your well-conceptualized, clear, and concise graphic will put you far ahead of other professionals who are not aware of the methodology in this book or fail to adhere to the "clean and simple" strategy.

You can also use the prefabricated graphics and themes built into PowerPoint. Remember, keep it clean and simple. PowerPoint offers a dizzying array of tacky effects that can destroy the integrity and clarity of a visual. Never add a "cool" effect because you think your graphic looks boring. Like accountants, programmers, and engineers, good designers have years of training and countless hours of experience. Adding "cool" effects without training will likely lead to a graphic that looks unprofessional and fails to achieve its primary objective. Over time, you will improve. The more graphics you create, the more comfortable and accomplished you will become. Adhere to the design principles in Chapter 3 and you will not go wrong.

On a case-by-case basis you can use outside images and photographs to support your graphic's primary objective. I've listed several resources on page 69. Additionally, use the virtual CD that came with this book as a starting point. It can help you and your team quickly build a library of easy-to-use, successful business graphics.

If you are creating a graphic for use in another software package, be sure to save your file as the appropriate file type for insertion into the software. Each application will have slightly different requirements. Determine what file types the software uses and save your graphic as that type. Remember to keep a copy of your PowerPoint source art for future edits. If you are supplying an editable copy of the graphic, be sure to avoid bullets, fonts, or any other visual elements that are not installed on the audience's computer.

2. LEVERAGE EXISTING GRAPHICS

The second strategy is leveraging existing graphics to create new, project-specific visuals. Your company or organization probably has existing graphics for standardized processes, often used tools, and/or frequently needed solutions to reoccurring tasks and issues. Start there. Aspects will need to be tailored for each project but referencing or starting with a depiction that has worked in the past is a smart move. Most authors struggle with thinking graphically. Attempting to develop the solution with no more than a blank sheet of paper or screen is unnecessarily challenging and time consuming. Instead, start with an existing image of a solution that worked in the past. This step will save hours and reduce stress, and the solution will be more thoughtful (benefiting from the evolution of the ideas/images as it is passed from one person or project to the next).

Picasso once said, "Good artists copy but great artists steal." I am not advocating the theft of other copyrighted graphics. Instead, be smart and leverage what others before you have learned. See what works and imitate it. Use the graphics in this book to discover applicable concepts and styles. These visuals have proven to be successful for business-related needs.

If possible, ask an experienced designer to create a library of frequently used graphic elements and types that you can easily edit as needed. Again, because of its ubiquity and relative low learning curve, I propose that you create your library in PowerPoint. If you are comfortable using higher-end graphics software, then I recommend Adobe Photoshop and Illustrator. Expect higher quality imagery from Adobe software, but the packages have a steeper learning curve and are used by far fewer business and technical professionals. If you only need advanced graphic design occasionally, hire a qualified design firm or designer to render the final version of the graphic you conceptualized. Alternatively, set up a Service Level Agreement (SLA) that grants you access to top talent whenever you need it.

QUICK NOTE

Are you unhappy with the limitations of Excel charts? Try tracing your Excel charts in PowerPoint. Use your Excel chart as your guide. (When rendering in PowerPoint, use a background grid. Use the Gridlines function or build it. To make a grid, start with one line and duplicate it. Use the Align, Distribute, and Rotate functions in PowerPoint to guarantee the ideal grid for your chart.)

QUICK NOTE

If editability is as important as high-end rendering, ask your design resource to create editable graphics in PowerPoint so you can tweak them for future use. (However, you will increase render time and may lose some quality by doing so.)

3. Evolve Your Concepts Before Rendering the Final Graphic

If you are low on time or money, make sure your concept is as far along as possible before rendering it (or assigning it to a designer). Sketch the solution first and, if applicable, present it to other subject matter experts for input. If everyone agrees that this is the best concept, the graphic can be rendered. If not, tweak the graphic on paper until everyone agrees. The graphic is then ready to be rendered on the computer.

"Our company will help build the foundation for AGA's successful future using four elements to manage and evolve the agency's existing infrastructure: people, process, technology, and knowledge."

4. Use a Template

A template is a key ingredient to quickly developing quality graphics and helps guarantee consistency. Consistency breeds trust. A template also eliminates the risk of a lengthy formatting pass on large projects. When you are working with a team, your template ensures that all graphics look as if one person or company created them. Follow your template. Choose a color palette, graphic style, arrow style, font, line spacing, and capitalization and stick with it.

It is imperative that your graphics are understandable. When choosing or creating your template be aware of the variables that affect the clarity of communication and need to be taken into consideration:

1) The size of the graphic presented
2) The medium on which it will be presented (poster board, on screen, etc.)
3) The knowledge of the audience regarding the subject matter
4) Special considerations (vision-impaired audience, graphics will be duplicated in black and white for review, etc.)

These variables determine what should be included and how to develop your template. For example, if your graphics are being projected onto a 10' screen using PowerPoint, size the graphic elements and text so your audience can easily read it from a distance. If graphic elements or labels are too small, your graphic may fail to accomplish its objective. Imagine spending thousands of dollars conceptualizing and rendering a graphic only to have your audience complain that they couldn't understand it because the text was too small to read. Use a template to determine what works best to quickly render successful graphics.

Avoid the use of cartoon-like or cheap clip art. In one instance, a government evaluator of a presentation given by a large company specifically stated in their review that the presentation's use of clip art (flat, "canned," usually uninspiring graphics) was a detriment to their proposal and led to a decision not to buy.

The overall style in which your graphics are rendered subconsciously communicates volumes about the presenter. In the following example, graphics A and B contain the same content but both communicate vastly different messages about the presenter. Which presenter's company, A or B, is larger? Which has more resources at their disposal? Which has the better solution? Graphic A says that you and/or your organization is professional, well-established, organized, and equipped to exceed expectations. Graphic B says that you and/or company is small and might lack the necessary resources. (The creator of graphic B failed to keep it clean and simple and ignored the value of using and adhering to a template.) There is no doubt that A is more appealing and memorable. Graphics A and B communicate the same surface (cognitive) information but each elicits different subsurface (emotional) responses.

QUICK NOTE

The rendering style should be consistent with the primary objective, audience, and subject matter. Avoid graphics like the following:

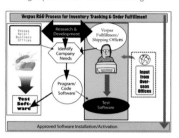

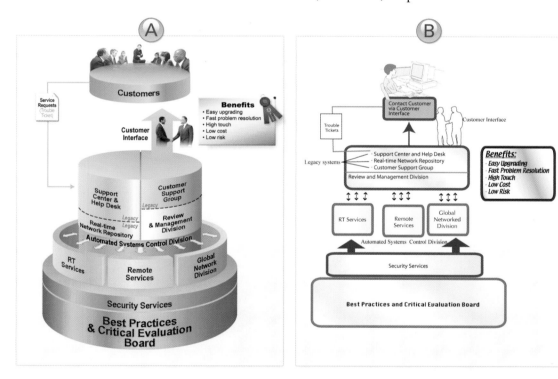

Additionally, the rendering style of your graphic also facilitates quicker dissemination of the data. If your goal is to efficiently communicate information, choose a relatively simplistic style similar to B in the following example.

QUICK NOTE

Experiments prove that aesthetically appealing graphic user interface designs are perceived to be easier to use than less appealing designs—whether they are easier to use or not. Aesthetic designs elicit positive feelings that result in a more tolerant and accepting user. Attractive interfaces positively influence the long-term experience of the user.

(Masaaki Kurosu and Kaori Kashimura, "Apparent Usability vs. Inherent Usability," *CHI '95 Conference Companion* [1995]: 292-293.

William Lidwell, Kritina Holden, and Jill Butler, *Universal Principles of Design*, Rockport Publishers [2003]: 18-19.)

QUICK NOTE

There are two types of graphics—vector and raster.

Vector graphics (think clip art) are resolution independent, which means they can be scaled without distortion. Vector images are easily manipulated and have a lower file size. Raster graphics (think photographs) are typically more visually appealing but are resolution dependent. Whichever you choose, avoid unprofessional looking imagery.

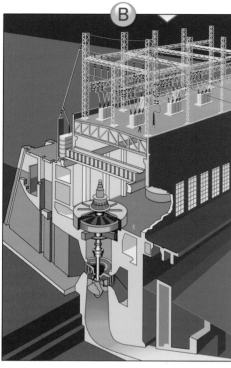

The following is an example of a simple one-page template for a PowerPoint presentation.

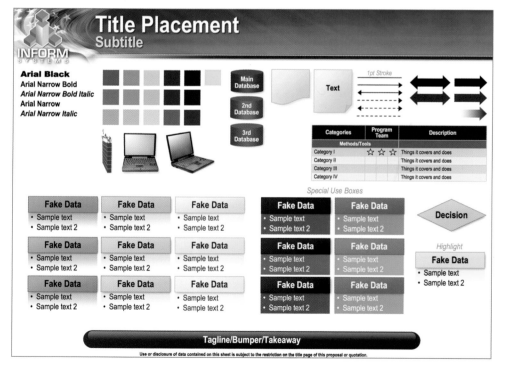

5. STORYBOARD

Create a storyboard when working on large projects. Agree to the story that you will tell before writing and developing graphics. Create graphics (or sketches) that address the solutions proposed for each of your major topics. Which of the following would be easier to reference?

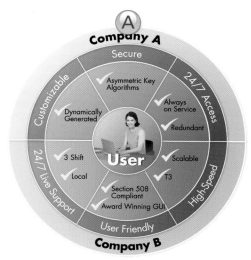

Company A Is Responsible for Tasks in Support of the User:
- Software Customizable by User
  - Dynamically Generated Information
- Security of Information Processed by the Software
  - Asymmetric Key Algorithms and Encrypted Information
- Reliable 24/7 Access to Software
  - Always on Service, Always Available to Users Worldwide
  - Redundant

Company B Is Responsible for Tasks in Support of the User:
- 24/7 Live User Technical Support
  - 3 Shifts of Technical Support Specialists
  - Uses Local Staff
- User Friendly Software
  - Compliant to Section 508 Regulations
  - Award-Winning Graphical User Interface
- High-Speed User Access
  - Scalable to Handle Increases in Demand, T3

Developing an overview graphic forces your team to analyze the information and organize it in a way that is logical, easy to follow, and makes it easier to write to and develop subsequent graphics. The more information revealed during storyboarding, the lower the risk of lengthy rewrites and wasted graphics. Finding a story and solution that everyone agrees to early in the process is a great way to get your graphics right the first time and save time and money.

6. MAKE YOUR GRAPHICS AUDIENCE FOCUSED

You **must** make the graphics audience focused. What is it about the information you are sharing that is personal and relevant to your audience? Make it obvious. Studies have proven that graphics communicate faster and are remembered better than text. Use this to your advantage. Highlight your features, benefits, and discriminators. Employing this strategy when creating graphics has proven invaluable to all who embrace it.

QUICK NOTE

Discriminators refer to what sets the solution or solution provider apart from the competition.

USING A GRAPHIC DESIGNER

If you have the luxury of using a professional designer, do it. When your design needs are unique and nothing on the market will suffice, use a professional, experienced designer. Be sure to communicate the P.A.Q.S. to the designer and explain your sketched concept. They may have suggestions for improvement. If you are working with a team, make the designer part of your team as early as possible. *Everyone* should share the same vision, mission, and goals for the project from the start.

Presenting a professionally rendered visual greatly impacts your success:

- It supports the presenter's competency, credibility, and professionalism. Essentially, it makes the presenter look better.

- It increases the likelihood of audience acceptance of the graphic. It looks professional; therefore, it is credible.

- It is more aesthetically appealing than a "doodle," and the audience will spend more time looking at it. They will be more likely to understand, remember, and be influenced by it.

Professionals who present at conferences and speaking events without compelling visuals are typically evaluated lower than those who do. Using professionally rendered graphics not only increases your audience's attention, understanding, and retention of the presented material, but also tells your audience that they are important enough to warrant extensive preparation and development.

Joan Miller (name changed), a proposal manager, taught a proposal writing course for over 10 years. The class began with students forming source selection teams to evaluate two proposals and choose a winner based on the established evaluation criteria. Proposal A was attractive, well written, and contained a large number of professionally rendered, visually appealing graphics, but the proposal was not compliant with the evaluation criteria. Proposal B was not well written, used a smaller number of dense, difficult to read graphics, but was compliant. If the source selection teams took the extra time needed to understand Proposal B's graphics, they would have found that the graphics suitably showed the system to be built. Not surprisingly, Miller often found that Proposal A (the easy-to-read, graphically appealing proposal) received the highest grades. When asked, the students said they were so caught up in the presentation that they failed to realize the proposal was not compliant.

Imagine receiving two competing lawn care service brochures. Lovely Lawn Care presents amateurish, clip art graphics. Miracle Lawn Care presents polished, professional graphics. Both companies use the same process. Based on the brochures, which is the better lawn care service company?

 QUICK NOTE

Aesthetic decisions, good or bad, form the audience's lasting impression of the company or person most associated with that graphic.

Most potential buyers would say Miracle Lawn Care is the better company. Now what if Miracle Lawn Care was more expensive than Lovely? Would clients pay more for the same service because of the professionalism and competency communicated by the polished, professional graphics? The answer is yes. Buying decisions based on image happen all the time. Companies sell the perception of professionalism, quality, superiority, and other attributes that motivate potential customers to buy their service or product. Much of the perception is created through the quality of their collateral materials, marketing materials, ads, website, business attire, office space, and anything that is customer facing. Companies know it is the overarching look of quality that significantly aids in the public's perception that it is a quality company. This applies to all audiences whether they are customers, potential customers, employees, investors, or the like. It becomes the company's responsibility to live up to the image it created or their efforts will be in vain.

Graphics have the power to communicate that a company is faster, stronger, better than its competition. Miracle Lawn Care instills trust and confidence in their abilities without ever speaking with potential buyers. You can do the same.

Professionally rendered graphics, if executed properly, exponentially increase your graphic's ability to influence your target audience. This book is full of key

 QUICK NOTE

"Resolution" is the quality of an image and "dimension" is the size of an image. Most printed graphics are 300 dpi (dots per inch—their resolution) unless they are vector images, which is resolution independent. Most web graphics are 72 dpi. Avoid using web graphics, especially in your printed materials. All web imagery is protected by copyright laws—although some sites grant permission for specified reuse—and at a resolution and dimension unsuitable for print.

QUICK NOTE

There are many design packages, but I have found that Adobe Photoshop, Illustrator, and Microsoft PowerPoint provide the most flexibility, the best results, and are used by most businesses and designers.

design principles that will help you render or *direct* the rendering of your winning graphic.

Do not ignore the quality of your final rendering. We are presented with an increasing amount of stimuli: television advertisements and shows, news, movies, magazines, billboards, telemarketers, radio spots, and websites all competing to get our attention. Some studies show that exposure to this increasing din of stimuli shrinks our attention spans. Your graphic needs to capture and hold your audience's attention and communicate the information quickly and precisely. If the audience has to study your image for too long they will lose interest. The audience may become frustrated and lose faith in the presenter.

CHAPTER 5: PROBLEM SOLVING—THREE TRAPS AND SEVEN RULES

THREE TRAPS

Many graphics fail for three reasons: too complicated, unclear, and poorly rendered. A visual becomes **too complicated** when the author attempts to convey too many messages in one graphic or includes too much detail.

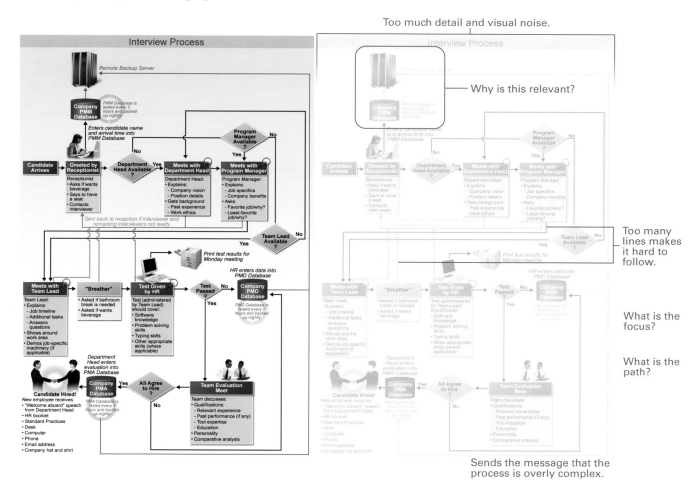

An **unclear** graphic, due to lack of identification and/or explanation, happens when the author erroneously assumes that their target audience understands the subject matter on the same level that he/she does. The following graphic fails to identify key elements and explain their meaning. The author assumed that their audience knew more about the subject matter than they did.

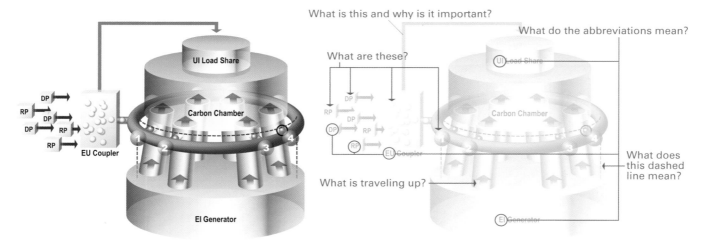

Poorly rendered graphics result in a host of negative outcomes. The worst of which are a loss of communication (or miscommunication) and the perception that the image and presenter are unprofessional.

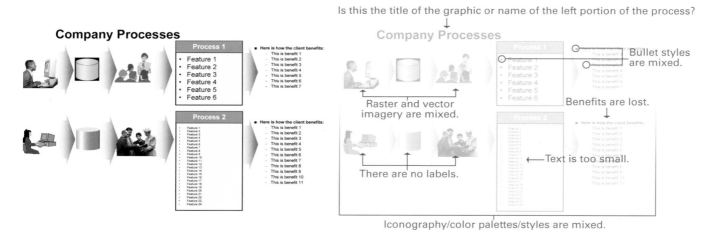

SEVEN RULES

The following seven rules will help you create successful graphics:

1) **All visual elements should have a specific role in the explanation and a reason for being chosen and incorporated.** This rule includes, but is not limited to, images, icons, symbols, shapes, colors, fonts, line weight, placement, and size. All aesthetic decisions should have a reason for being chosen that contributes to your graphic's primary objective.

2) **Stay consistent.** Internal consistency cultivates a feeling of trust because it indicates to the audience that the information presented was designed through careful consideration. Inconsistency breeds confusion. Changes in graphic style, color, shape, and iconography without your target audience's understanding of the change results in miscommunication. If a change occurs at any point (element to element or graphic to graphic) and no reason is given, confusion is the likely outcome. Alternatively, your audience may link an unintended meaning to the change. For example, changing the color of one box in a graphic indicates to your audience that this box is different. Why? Did you explain the difference? Is it obvious? Is it important? Do not add variables where none are needed. Never assume your audience knows the reason or understands the relevance. Clearly define and establish relevancy of any change in consistency.

3) As Edward Tufte, Professor Emeritus at Yale University and writer of seven information design books, said, "**Getting it right is far more important than being original.** Successful graphics explain that which is intended. Being innovative at the cost of clarity is not an option."

4) **Keep it clean and simple.** Unnecessary visual clutter and too much data interfere with audience understanding. Focus on the most important questions your audience has. You cannot achieve the primary objective if your target audience cannot quickly digest your visual or is confused by the graphic. If your graphic is too verbose or complex, suggest using another standalone graphic to communicate what could not be included in one visual. Avoid using too many different images, lines, shapes, patterns, textures, and colors. Doing so helps eliminate unnecessary visual noise that interferes with your graphic's primary objective. Align your shapes and lines to a grid to communicate that you and your organization offer structure. It also ensures that your graphic is easier to disseminate.

   Ockham's Razor, a widely accepted and proven postulate, asserts that simplicity in all design is preferred over complexity. Unnecessary visual complexity increases the likelihood of audience misinterpretation, confusion, and unintended consequences. This principle does not mean that all design should be devoid of aesthetic considerations and embellishments such as colors, gradients, textures, and shadows—it depends upon the objectives. When presenting a graphic that has the

QUICK NOTE

"Let thy speech be short, comprehending much in a few words."

(William Shakespeare)

Simple designs are easier
to understand. Compare the
old and new New York City
Subway maps below:

singular objective to convey data and nothing more, use the least amount of aesthetic embellishment.

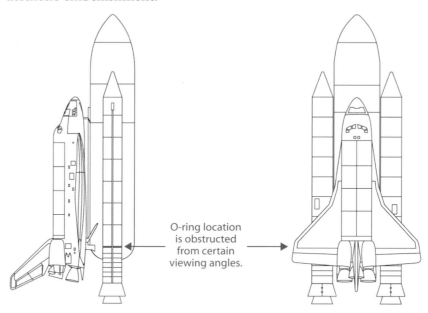

O-ring location is obstructed from certain viewing angles.

There are some instances where seemingly challenging or cluttered graphics are easily read and digested by the target audience. For example, an Earned Value Management System (EVMS) graphic might be confusing to most but would be very clear to those who have learned to read such graphical data. To the trained viewer, the following information graphic shows a risk probability schedule. It quickly communicates how potential changes in budget at different milestones can have a ripple effect on future costs.

Earned Value Management System (EVMS)

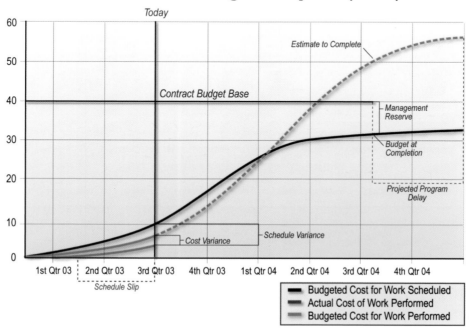

As always, do your homework. Before developing and presenting specialty graphic types, icons, symbols, or imagery, be sure your audience understands what it is you are communicating.

The "10 Second Rule" has helped me create successful business graphics. There are several interpretations but I find this definition most applicable: **If your target audience doesn't know and understand the main point of your graphic within 10 seconds, the graphic will probably fail to achieve its primary objective.** In many instances you have far less than 10 seconds. Your goal is to communicate as quickly and clearly as possible.

Unfortunately, I have seen a cluttered, dense, hard-to-understand visual achieving the primary objective, especially in business graphics. Perhaps the target audience needed that level of detail to understand the concept being presented. However, it is more likely that the audience ignored the lack of clarification and/or explanation. The audience may have chosen this potentially flawed path of reasoning: "The graphic looks good. It has all the terms and elements I needed to see. It looks as complicated as a solution to this problem should be. I don't feel like figuring it out anymore. I've heard this company is trustworthy. It seems good enough to me. Let's move forward." Or perhaps the audience felt that if they asked for clarification they would appear unintelligent. Whatever the reason, although the graphic failed to communicate all intended messages, it succeeded in its primary objective. The graphic used what I call *"razzle dazzle"*—when the author or designer, purposefully or not, uses attractive or dense visuals or a complicated layout rather than focusing on the audience's need to understand. Was the graphic successful? Only if their goal was to confuse the audience and hope they reached a decision that coincided with the primary objective. This is a poor, potentially unethical tactic.

5) **Label elements directly to avoid confusion.** When depicting steps in a process, label them as such. The clearer your labels, the more effective your clarification and/or explanation. As a result, your graphic is more likely to be successful. Avoid legends. Legends add visual clutter and force the audience to waste valuable time deciphering your message.

6) **Use recognizable imagery** or quickly identify and explain any unknown imagery. If an image is introduced that is not recognized, understood, or quickly defined, the intended messages will be clouded or lost. For example, never show a low resolution, dark, or out-of-focus image that may not be identified or could be misinterpreted as something else. Additionally, never show an image of a very technical component such as a valve switch to an audience that may not know what a valve switch is or does. If a new action, concept, or entity must be introduced, define it. Share its relevance with your target audience.

QUICK NOTE

There is an exception to every rule ... Use cognitive dissonance to increase your audience's attention during an oral presentation. Make a graphic that is *seemingly* disconnected or incongruent with the subject matter. Your graphic should be unpredictable and require a verbal explanation to connect the dots. Give your audience just enough information in the graphic to peak their interest. Essentially, you are giving them a puzzle to solve or teasing them with a portion of the information they need. Beware, this strategy can backfire if your graphic is not thoughtful, thought provoking, or offers no benefit when the connection is revealed.

7) **Focus on your audience.** Solve your audience's unique challenges. Make your graphic personal and relevant. Make it obvious that the information is important and valuable and is linked to their wants and needs.

Do not simply share history, facts, and figures about you or your company (the presenter). Show your audience why it matters. Explain how they benefit. Give them a reason to care. Tell your audience how they benefit **first**, then prove how it will be done. Link features to benefits. Do this and your graphic will stand out. Every other company says they are customer-focused. What company doesn't say they offer the highest quality, the best solution, and the greatest value? It is estimated that every three years the amount of business information prospects and customers process to make a decision doubles.[1] Make it easier for them. See it from your audience's point-of-view. Make them *want* to see what you have to offer. Make the benefits the driving force behind your graphic.

When applicable, point out the discriminators. Why are you or your company uniquely qualified to help the audience? In the graphic, point out what makes you the best choice. Tie discriminators to features and benefits. Show your audience the special connection between the solution provider and their solution.

Focusing on your audience forces you to conceptualize and render your graphic using information, terms, and imagery in a way that they understand. Putting your audience first has a significant impact on the final visual and *greatly* increases the likelihood of your success.

---

1. Bill Jensen, *Simplicity*, (New York, NY: Perseus Publishing, 2000), 11.

CHAPTER 6:
GRAPHIC TYPES

QUICK NOTE

If you like the graphics
in this book or want to
see more examples, go to
BizGraphicsOnDemand.com.
Graphics are available for
immediate download and are
editable in PowerPoint 2007
or newer. All graphics can be
brought into MS Word, Adobe
products, as well as most
software.

Experience is the best teacher. Studying and reviewing field-tested examples is the second best way to learn how to create successful graphics. Although the content has been changed, each of the graphic types and styles in this chapter were successfully used in real-life presentations to explain, clarify, and support the presenter's mission.

Use these examples to increase your graphic vocabulary. Let the examples be your roadmap to conceptualize and render the right graphic for the right need. Most of the graphic elements in the following examples are interchangeable. Mix and match graphic types as you see fit.

Many of the graphic types, titles, and descriptions/applications in this book are not absolute. They are, however, graphic types used most often in business communications, presentations, marketing, proposals, websites, and multimedia. Based on your needs, add to this library or develop your own graphic types. For example, I found that a puzzle is an excellent metaphor to describe many elements coming together to form a new whole. Because I frequently encounter the need for puzzle graphics, I added that visual solution to this library of graphic types. Use this core collection as a starting point to create your own unique graphic database.

Area Chart

A graphic that depicts continuous quantitative data usually over time and uses filled areas to communicate amounts, time frames, or values.

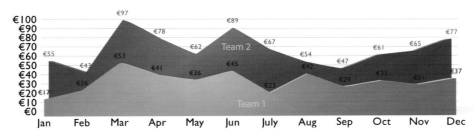

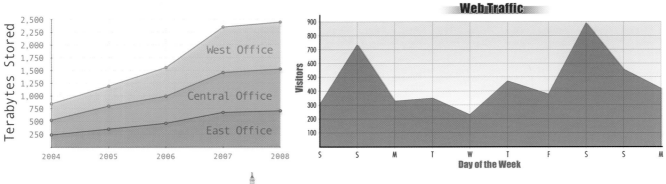

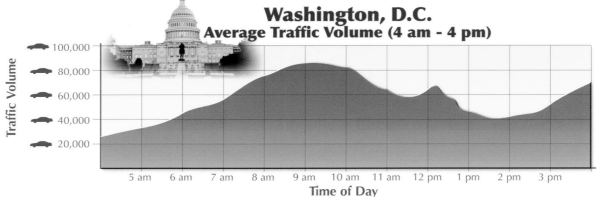

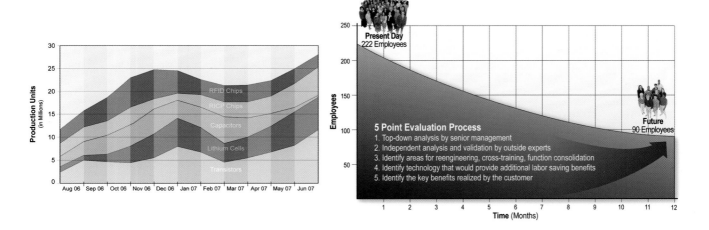

BAR CHART

A graphic that depicts the changes in quantitative data using "bars," where the size of each bar represents the proportional value of the quantitative data.

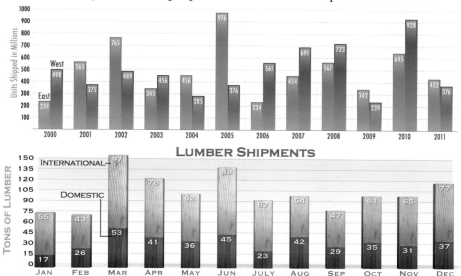

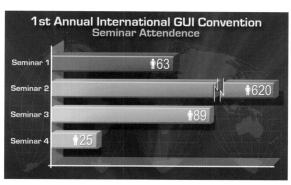

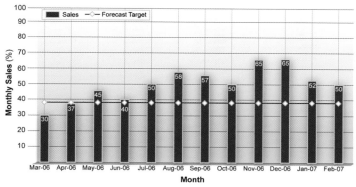

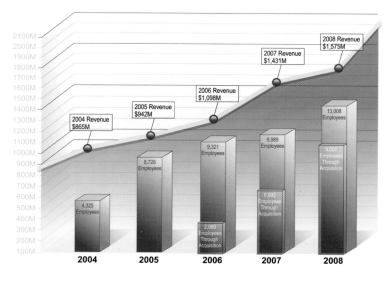

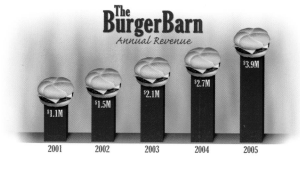

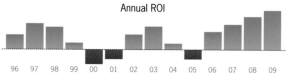

Before and After Graphic

A graphic that compares the "as is" or "before" state to the "to be" or "after" state.

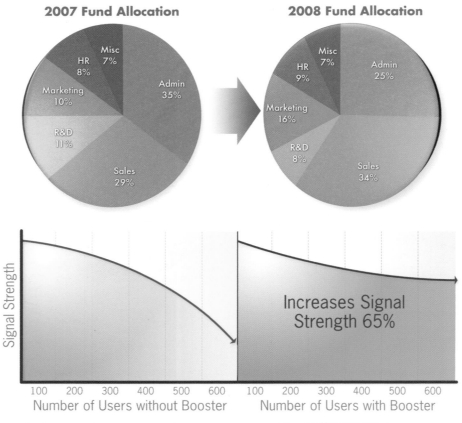

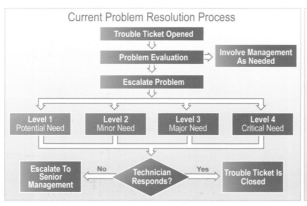

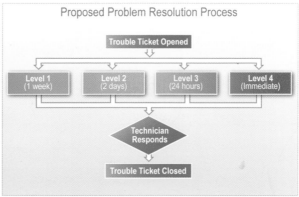

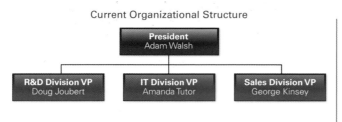

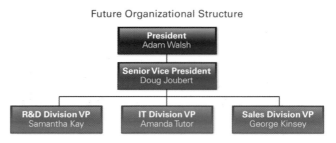

Bridge Graphic

A graphic metaphor depicting the connection or transition between two actions, concepts, or entities.

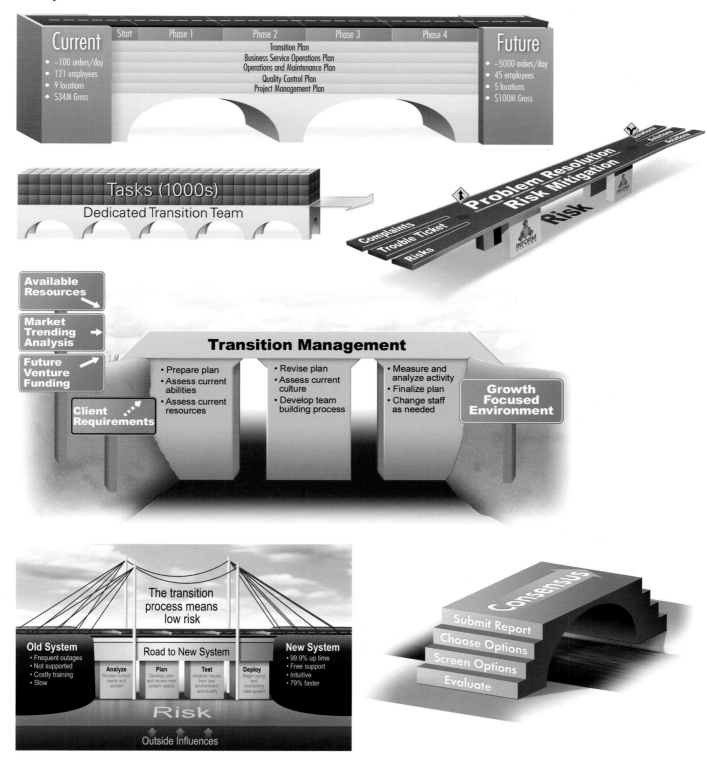

BUBBLE CHART

A graphic that uses circles or spheres to show ranges of quantitative data. It can also illustrate the uncertainty of predicted value.

Bubble size represents percent of market share

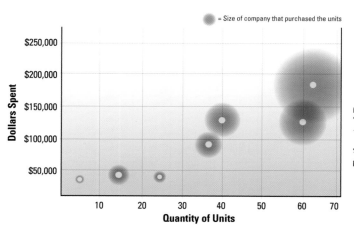

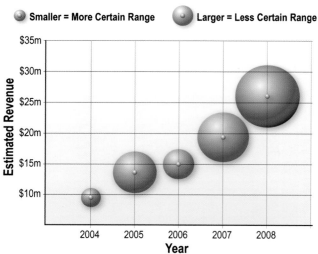

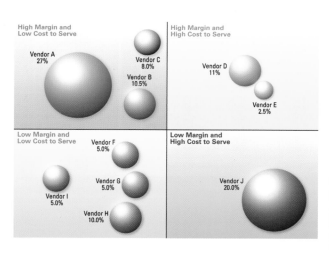

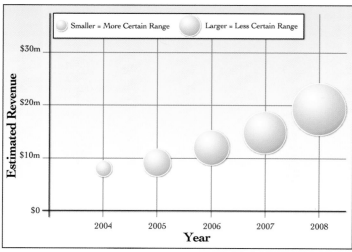

BUILDING BLOCKS

A graphic that interconnects data to illustrate how elements work together to create a larger unit.

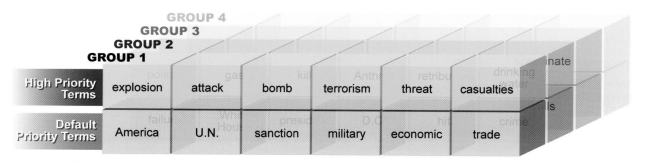

CALENDAR

A table showing years (or a year), months, weeks, and days.

Sunday	Monday	Tuesday	Wednesday	Thursday	Friday	Saturday
		1 Production Request Received	2 Production Request Processed	3	4 Production Request Approved	5
6	7 Production Kick-off Meeting	8	9 Production	10	11	12
13	14	15 Production	16	17	18	19
20	21 Production Review Meeting	22 Production Finalized	23	24	25 Product Inspected and Tested	26
27	28	29	30 Product Delivered to Customer	31		

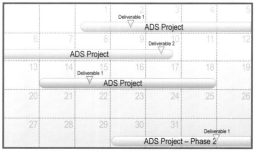

CANDLESTICK CHART

A chart traditionally used to analyze values and sales of stocks, bonds, commodities, etc. Price is shown in the vertical axis and time in the horizontal axis.

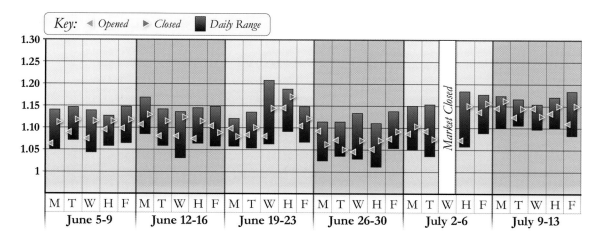

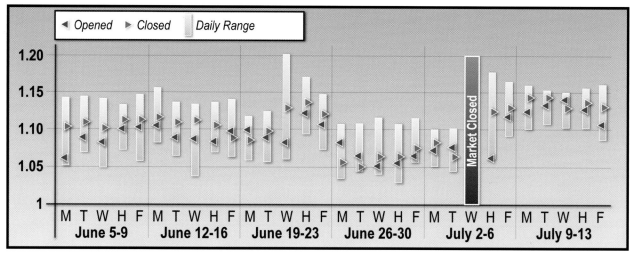

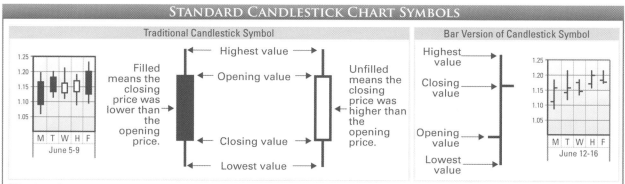

Warning: Be sure the symbols are understood. Candlestick chart symbols are not universally known. Because of this fact I created a version of the candlestick chart (seen above) that is more communicative to a larger audience. However, if the target audience is accustomed to the industry standards, use the appropriate symbols.

Circle Charts

A family of graphics that display quantitative data using a circular format and includes radar graphs, sector graphs, circle column graphs, and many similarly shaped graphics.

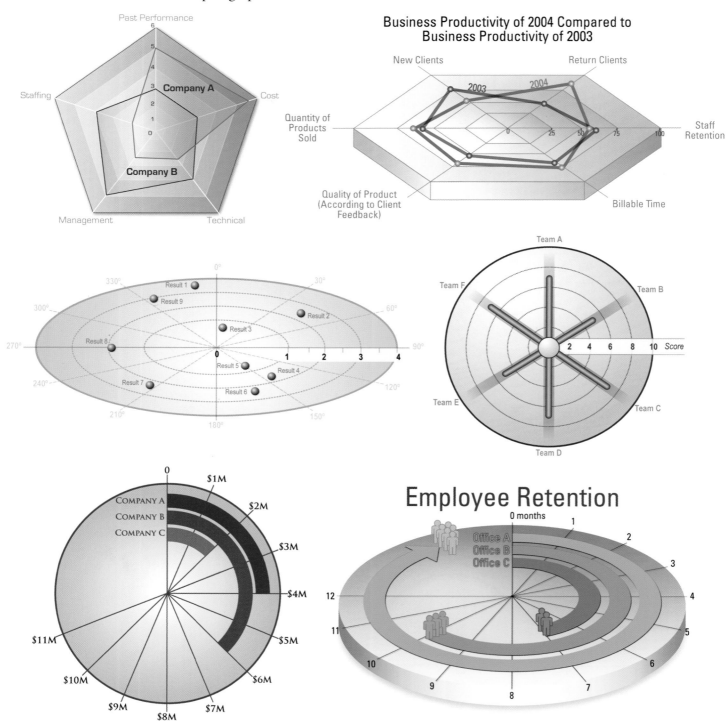

COLLAGE

A graphic that is composed of juxtaposed images.

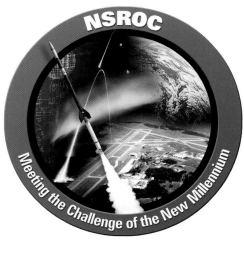

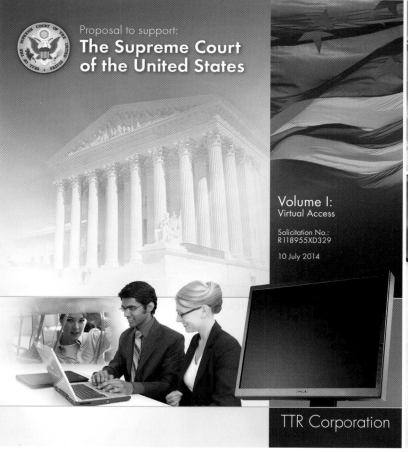

CONVEYOR BELT GRAPHIC

A graphic metaphor that depicts a repeatable linear process.

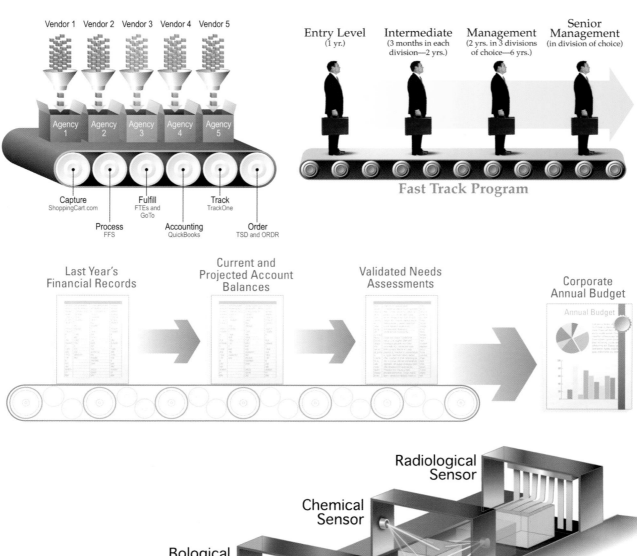

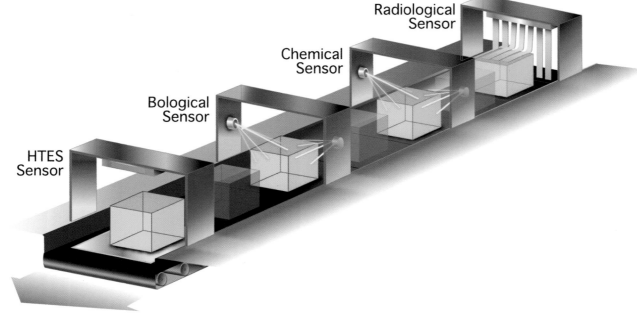

CROSS SECTION DIAGRAM

A graphic where an entity or depiction of a concept is cut in half so the different layers that make up the whole can be viewed and individually defined.

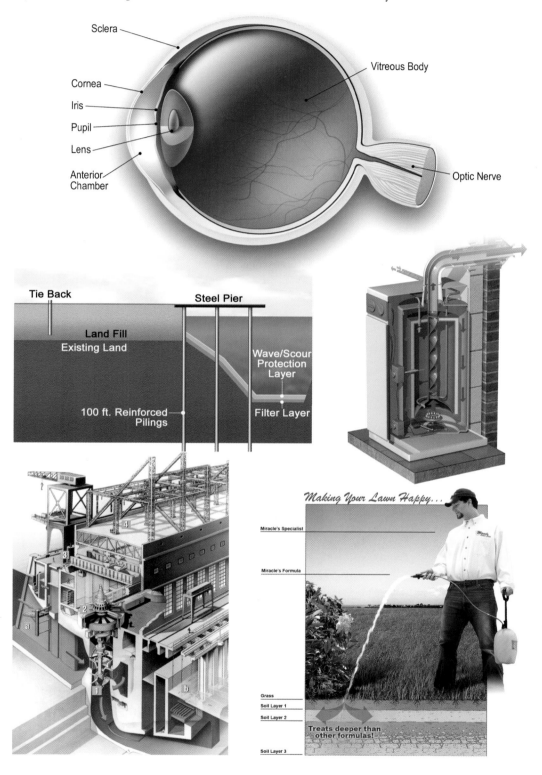

Sclera

Vitreous Body

Cornea

Iris

Pupil

Lens

Anterior Chamber

Optic Nerve

Tie Back

Steel Pier

Land Fill
Existing Land

Wave/Scour Protection Layer

100 ft. Reinforced Pilings

Filter Layer

Making Your Lawn Happy...

Miracle's Specialist

Miracle's Formula

Grass
Soil Layer 1
Soil Layer 2

Treats deeper than other formulas!

Soil Layer 3

Cutaway Diagram

This graphic is similar to a cross section diagram where you can see the inner workings or mechanics of an entity or depiction of a concept viewed through a missing or transparent portion of the outermost layer.

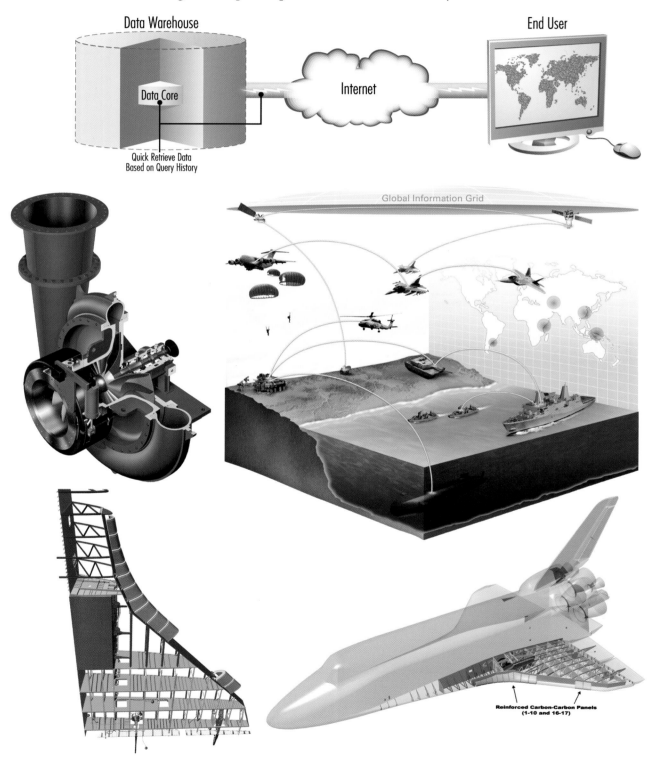

DASHBOARD GRAPHIC

A graphic that presents multiple metrics—potentially using multiple graphic types—in one consolidated format. (Think of you car's dashboard.)

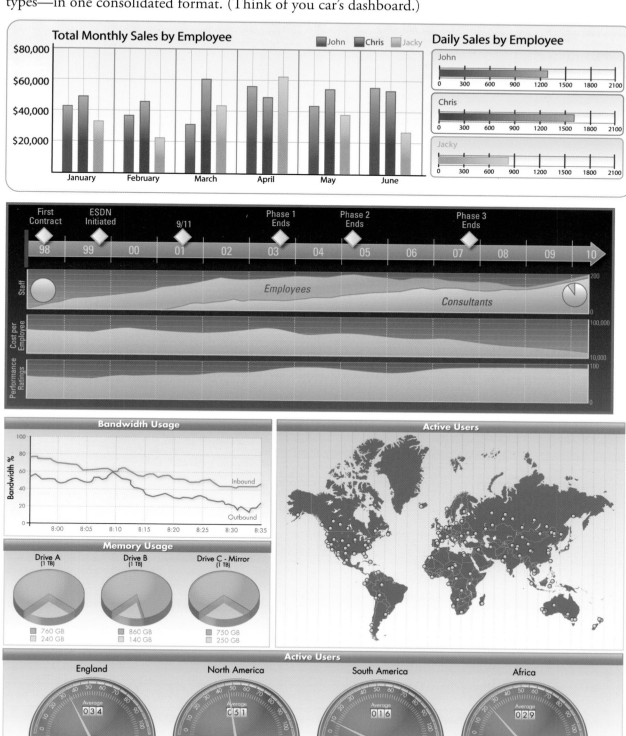

DOME GRAPHIC

A graphic that looks like a "snow globe" illustrating the containment of elements. (The dome graphic is especially good at communicating protection/security.)

EXPLODED DIAGRAM

A graphic showing the disassembled parts of an entity or concept placed in a manner that indicates their relative positions when reassembled.

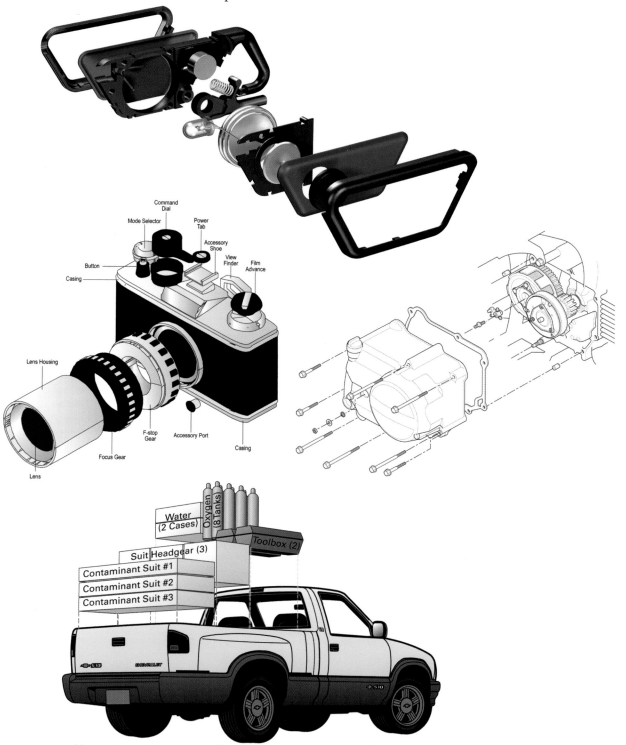

Command Dial

Mode Selector

Power Tab

Accessory Shoe

View Finder

Film Advance

Button

Casing

Lens Housing

F-stop Gear

Accessory Port

Casing

Focus Gear

Lens

Water (2 Cases)

Oxygen (8 Tanks)

Toolbox (2)

Suit Headgear (3)

Contaminant Suit #1

Contaminant Suit #2

Contaminant Suit #3

Hazardous Response Equipment Layout for Chevy S10

Floor Plan

A graphic depicting the layout of a room(s) or level(s) in a building.

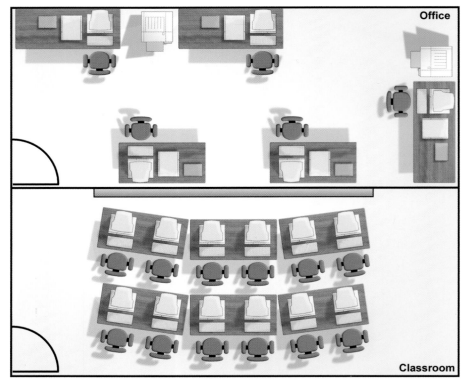

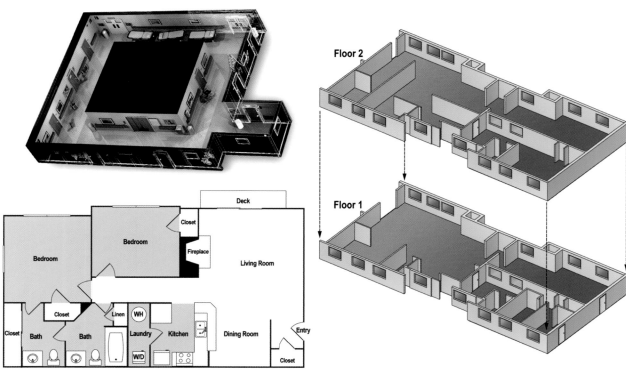

FUNNEL GRAPHIC

A graphic metaphor showing the passing of elements through a conduit (the funnel) resulting in the effective allocation, consolidation, and/or organization of those elements.

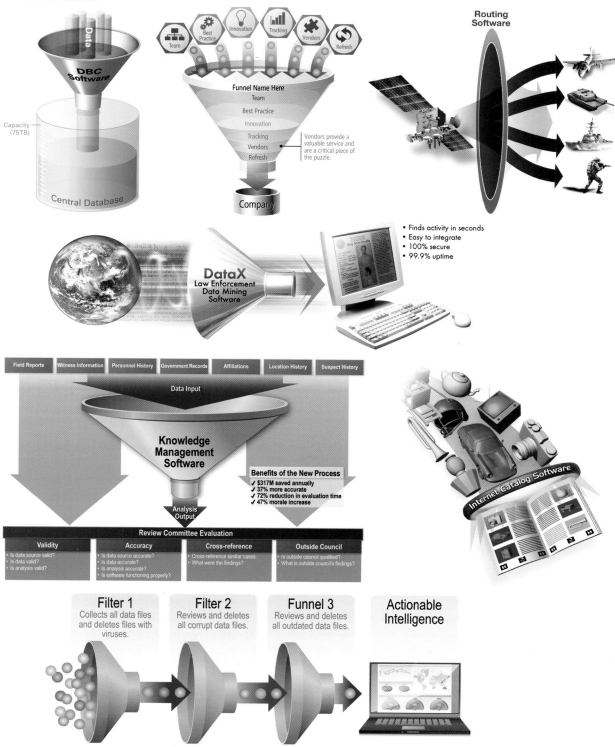

GANTT CHART

A bar chart representing time and activity used for planning, tracking, and controlling schedules.

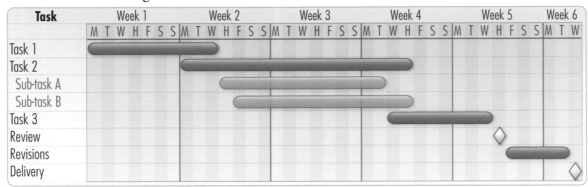

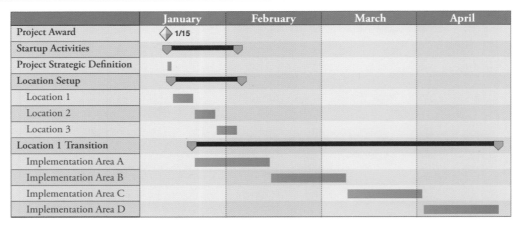

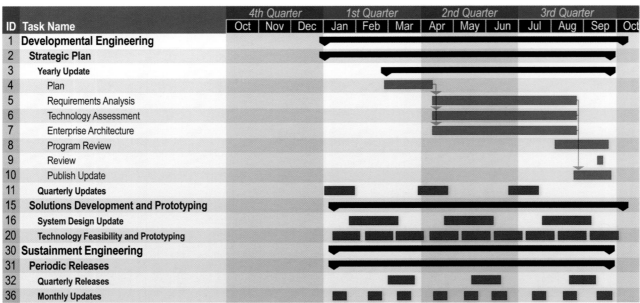

Gauge Graphic

A graphic metaphor using readouts and measurement tools to depict data for analysis.

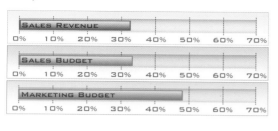

Daily Sales

Monthly Sales
(in thousands)

GEAR GRAPHIC

A graphic metaphor depicting how parts work together and often illustrates processes and interoperability.

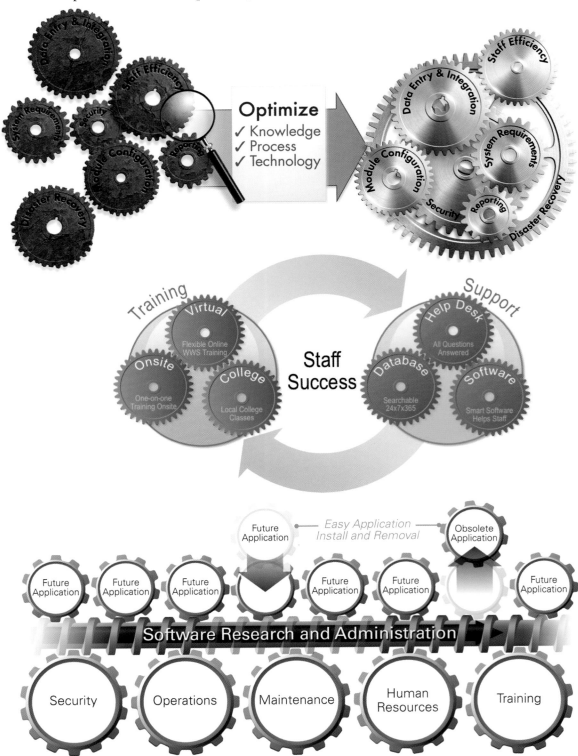

ILLUSTRATION

A visual representation that is used to make the subject more appealing or easier to understand. (Illustrations are often used when a photograph is not an option.)

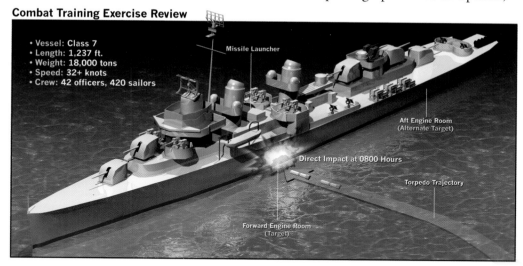

Combat Training Exercise Review

- Vessel: Class 7
- Length: 1,237 ft.
- Weight: 18,000 tons
- Speed: 32+ knots
- Crew: 42 officers, 420 sailors

Missile Launcher

Aft Engine Room
(Alternate Target)

Direct Impact at 0800 Hours

Torpedo Trajectory

Forward Engine Room
(Target)

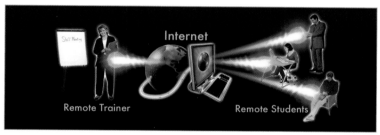

Internet

Remote Trainer

Remote Students

HIPAA Security Regulations

GAP

Existing Environment

LINE CHART

A graphic showing the changes in quantitative data using lines, where the position of a line represents the proportional value of the data.

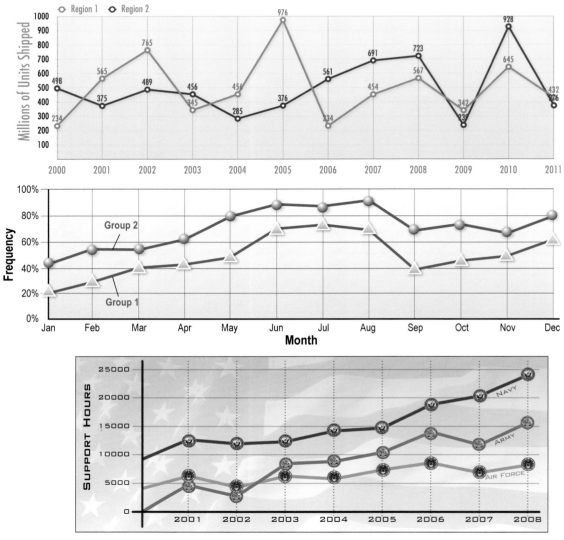

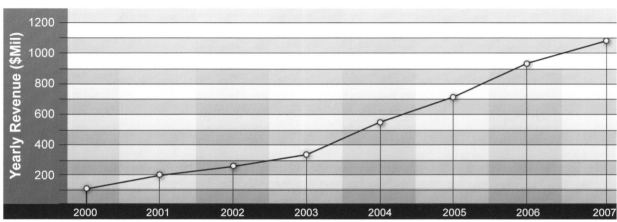

LOOPING GRAPHIC

A graphic that depicts a repeating process or event.

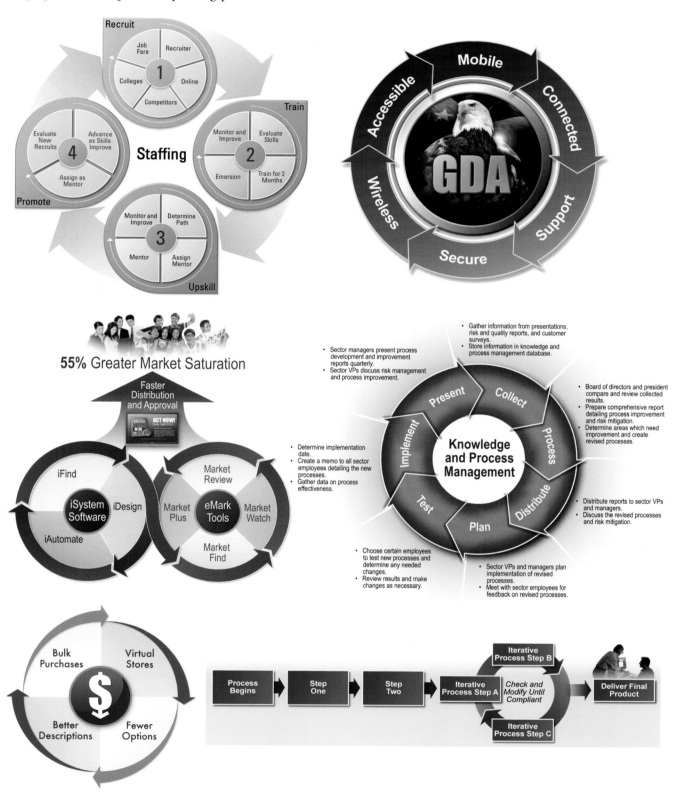

Map Graphic

A graphic showing a region of physical space: a continent, country, city, office building, etc.

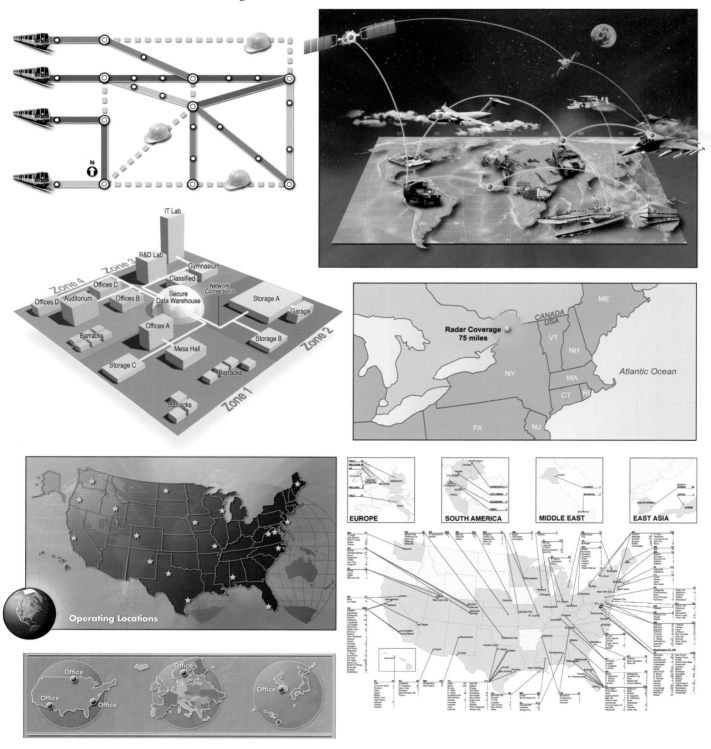

Network Diagram

A diagram showing the connections between elements that compose a network.

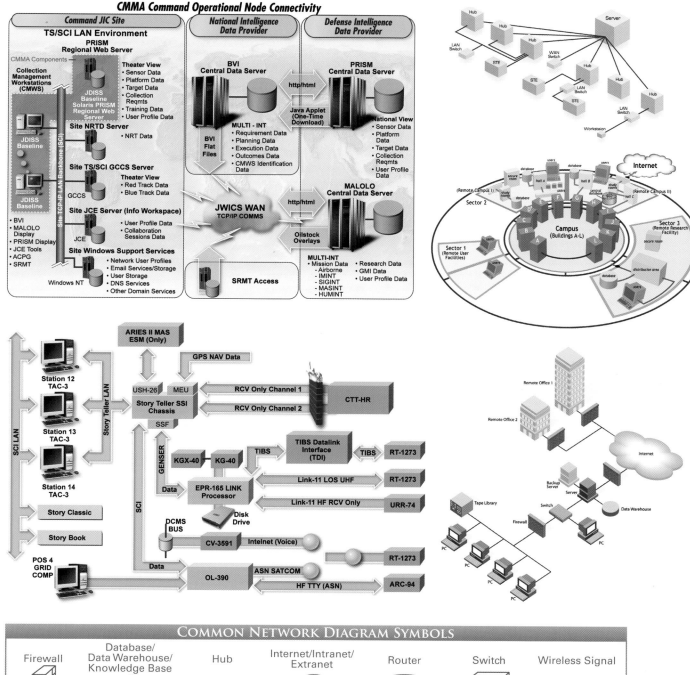

Warning: Be sure the symbols are understood. There are many more network diagram symbols. In my experience, the average viewer does not know or remember the meanings of many other symbols.

Organizational Chart

A graphic depicting the hierarchy, arrangement, structure, and/or relationship of a group of elements. (Typically, an organization and its personnel are the subject matter.)

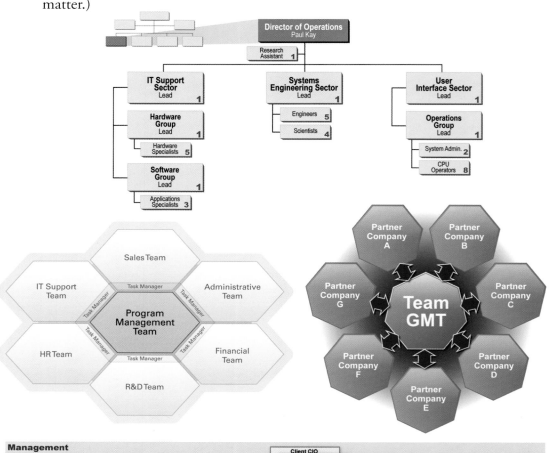

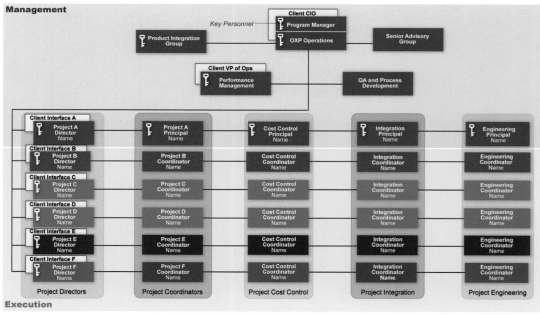

Peg Graphic

A graphic showing the interconnectivity of entities or ideas to create a unified whole (think Legos®).

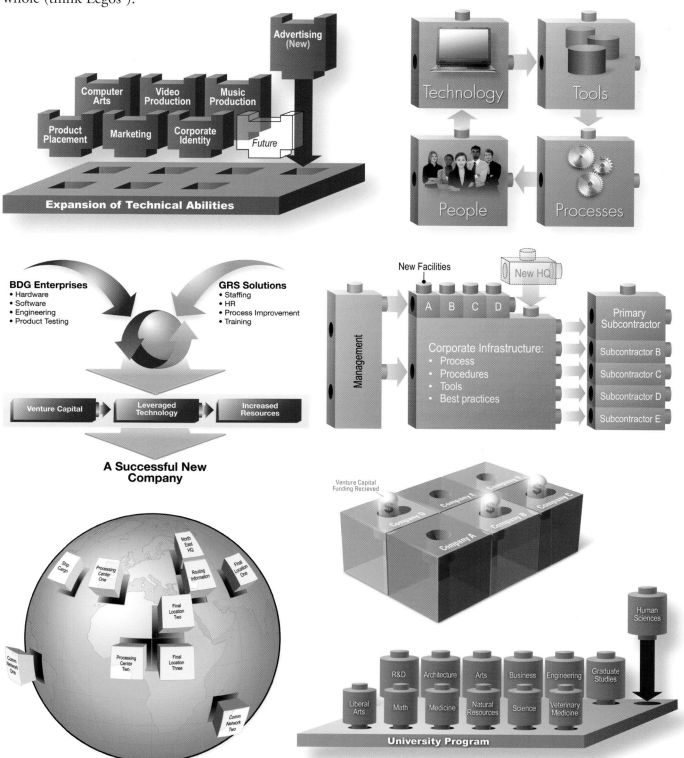

PHOTOGRAPH

A picture of a person, place, or thing.

F-16

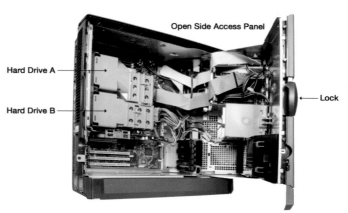

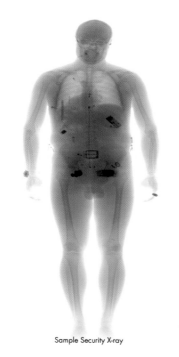

Sample Security X-ray

Video cameras monitor all frequently used illegal entry points into the U.S. at the Border Patrol's Communications Center near Yuma, Arizona.

PIE CHART (OR SEGMENTED CHART)

A graphic that communicates percentages of the whole using proportional segments.

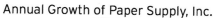
Annual Growth of Paper Supply, Inc.

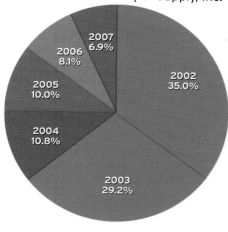

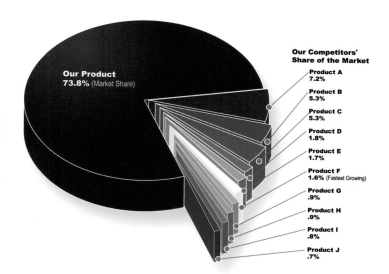

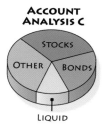

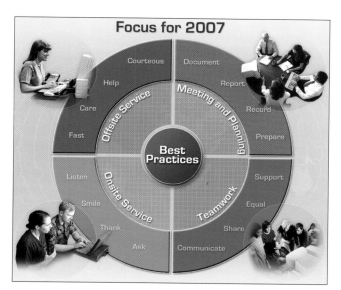

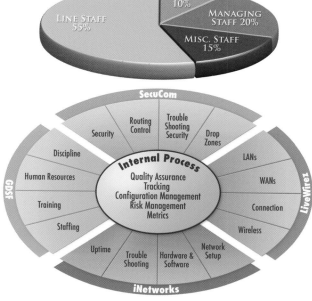

PIPE GRAPHIC

A graphic metaphor representing the isolated linear flow of elements.

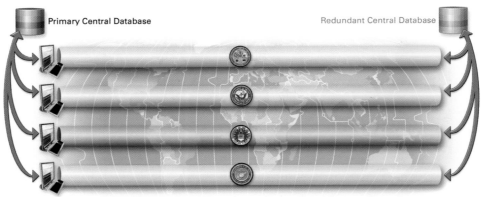

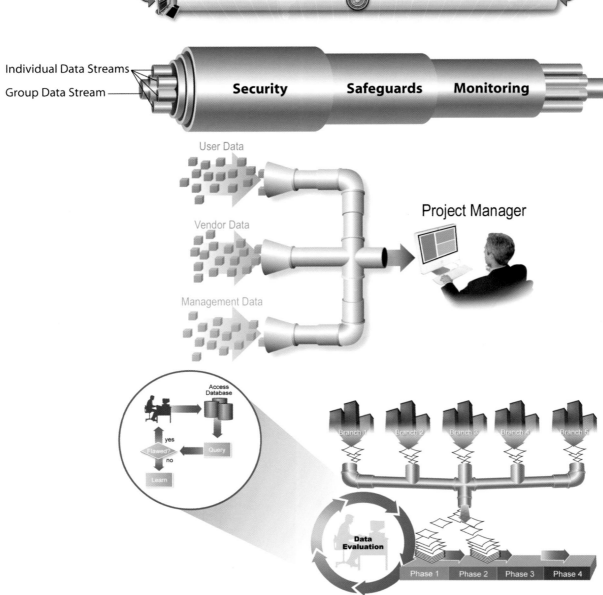

POINT CHART

A graphic that shows quantitative data using plotted points.

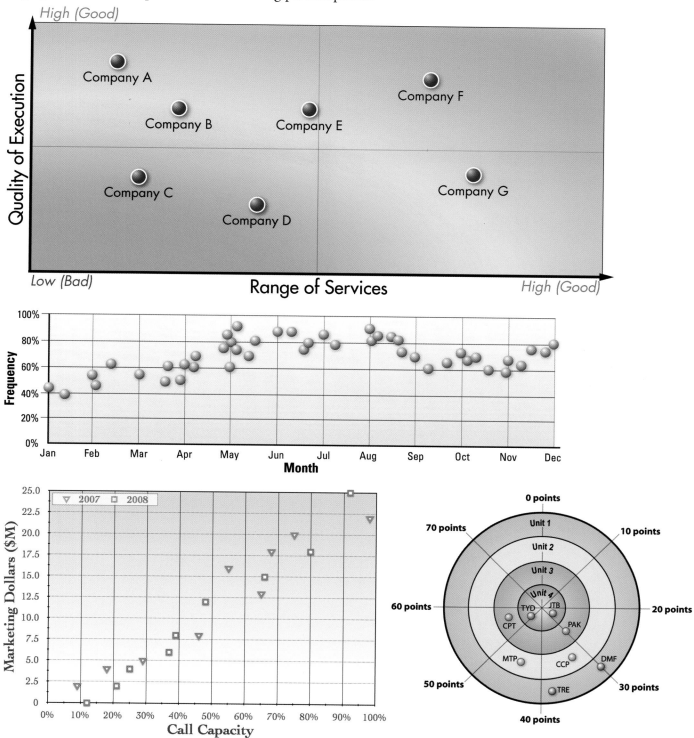

PROCESS DIAGRAM (OR FLOW CHART)

A graphic showing the flow or progression of steps in a process or event.

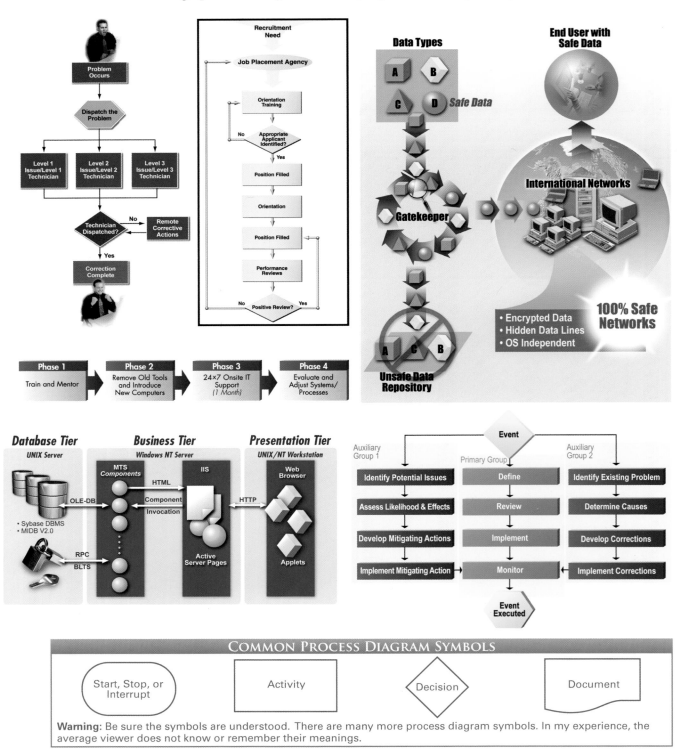

PUZZLE GRAPHIC

A graphic metaphor representing the synergy of separate elements that creates a
new whole.

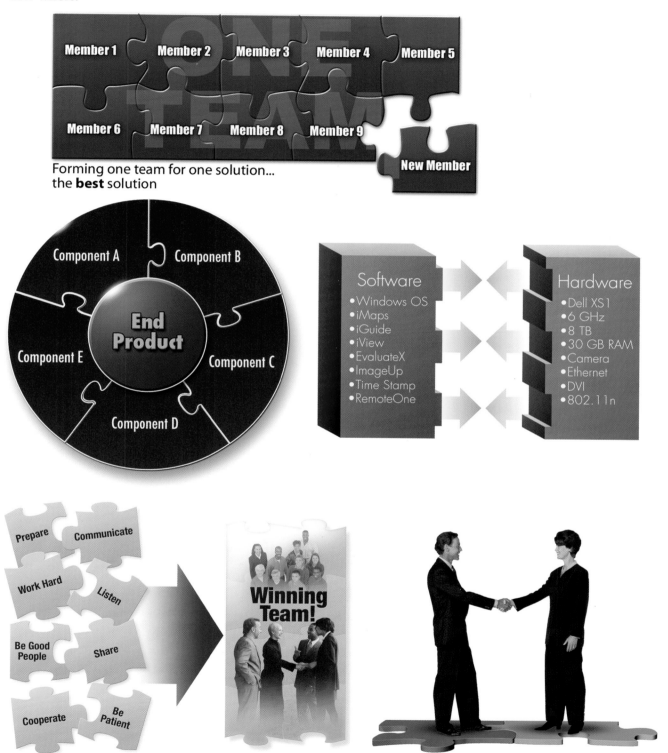

Pyramid Graphic

A graphic metaphor that depicts hierarchy, arrangement, structure, and/or relationship of a group of elements. The bottom elements support the elements above.

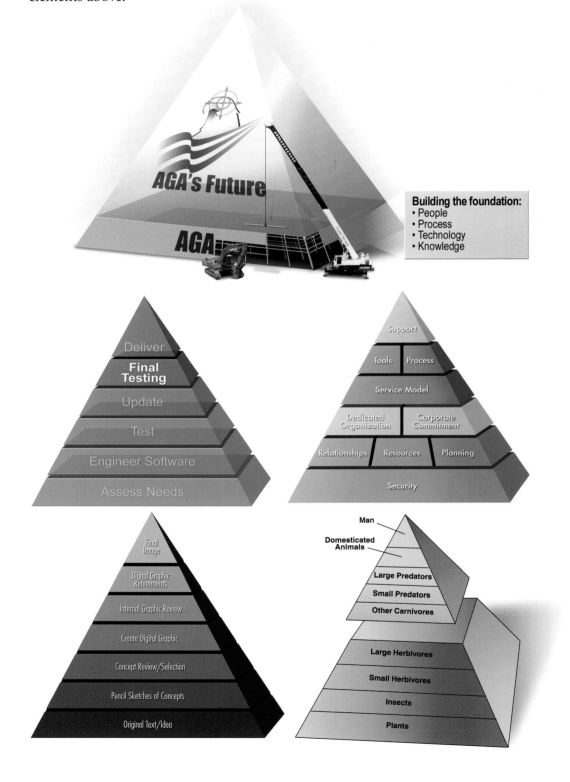

RISK MATRIX

A table that depicts varying levels of risk as affected by the influences of one or more variables.

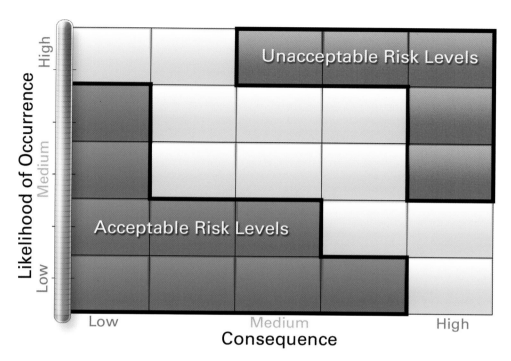

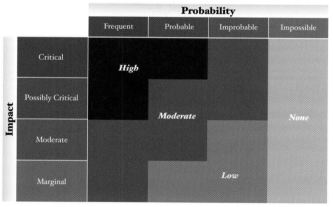

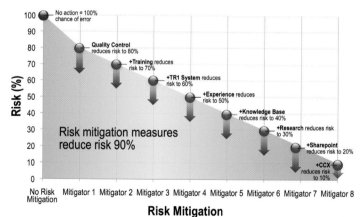

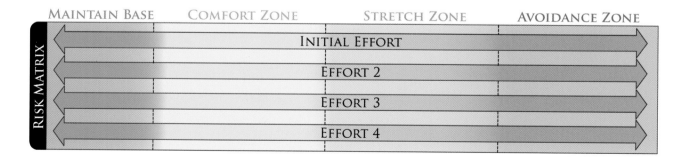

ROAD GRAPHIC (OR PATH GRAPHIC)

A graphic metaphor depicting the path between the "as is" or "before" state to the "to be" or "after" state.

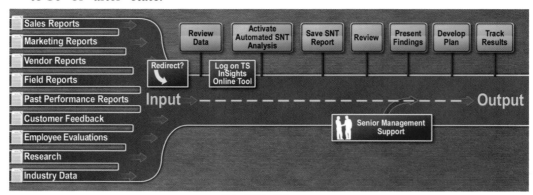

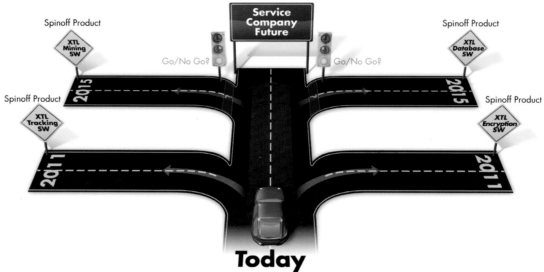

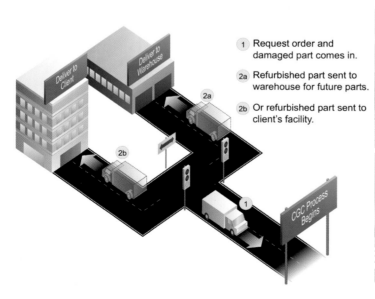

1. Request order and damaged part comes in.

2a. Refurbished part sent to warehouse for future parts.

2b. Or refurbished part sent to client's facility.

SCALE GRAPHIC

A graphic metaphor that illustrates comparison.

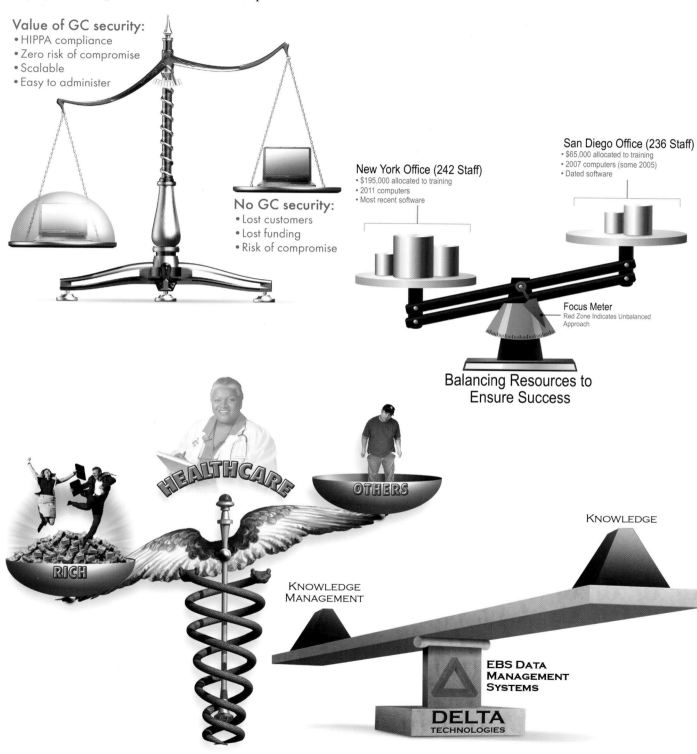

Value of GC security:
- HIPPA compliance
- Zero risk of compromise
- Scalable
- Easy to administer

No GC security:
- Lost customers
- Lost funding
- Risk of compromise

New York Office (242 Staff)
- $195,000 allocated to training
- 2011 computers
- Most recent software

San Diego Office (236 Staff)
- $65,000 allocated to training
- 2007 computers (some 2005)
- Dated software

Focus Meter
Red Zone Indicates Unbalanced Approach

Balancing Resources to Ensure Success

HEALTHCARE

OTHERS

RICH

KNOWLEDGE

KNOWLEDGE MANAGEMENT

EBS DATA MANAGEMENT SYSTEMS

DELTA TECHNOLOGIES

SPIRAL GRAPHIC

A graphic metaphor that illustrates the evolution of an action, concept, or entity through a cyclical process.

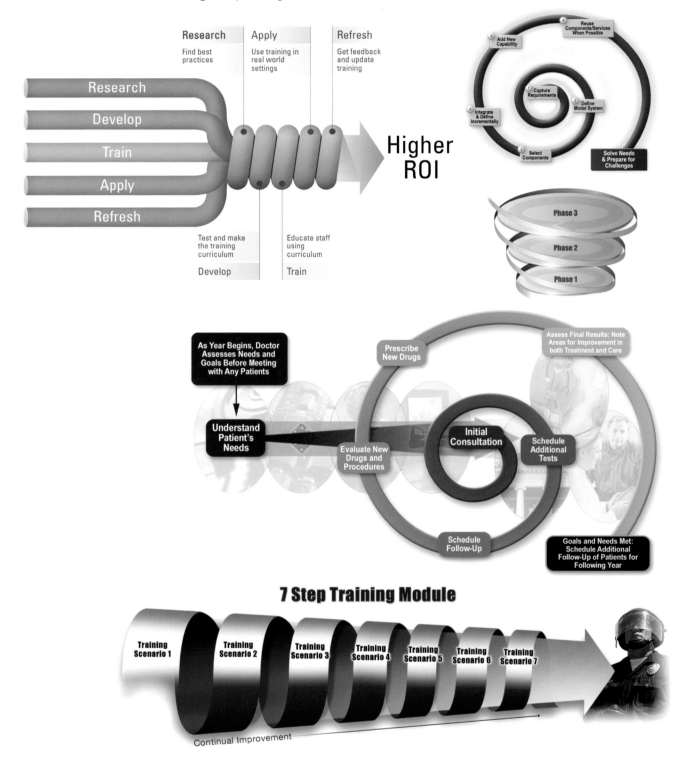

STACKED DIAGRAM

A graphic that depicts the hierarchy, arrangement, structure, and/or relationship of a group of elements. A stacked diagram can also show flow or a progression of steps in a process similar to a pyramid and/or process diagram but can be more versatile.

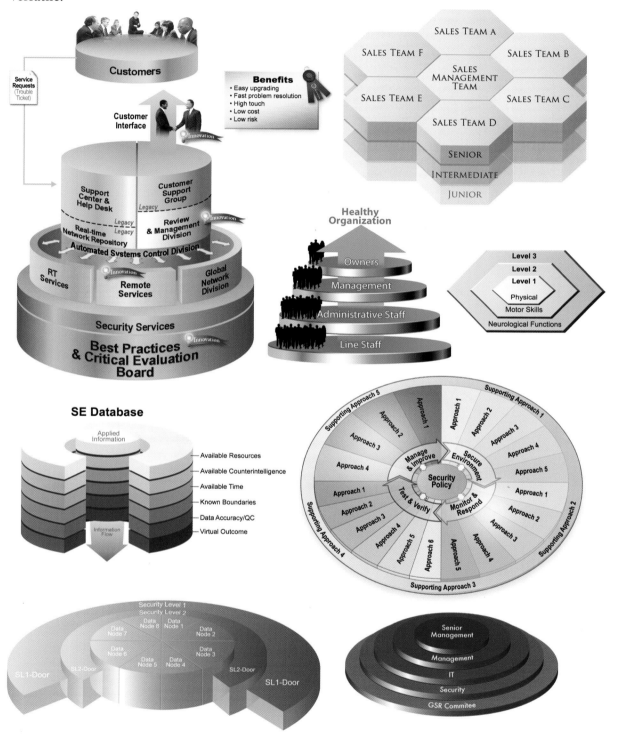

STAIR GRAPHIC

A graphic metaphor depicting steps in a process.

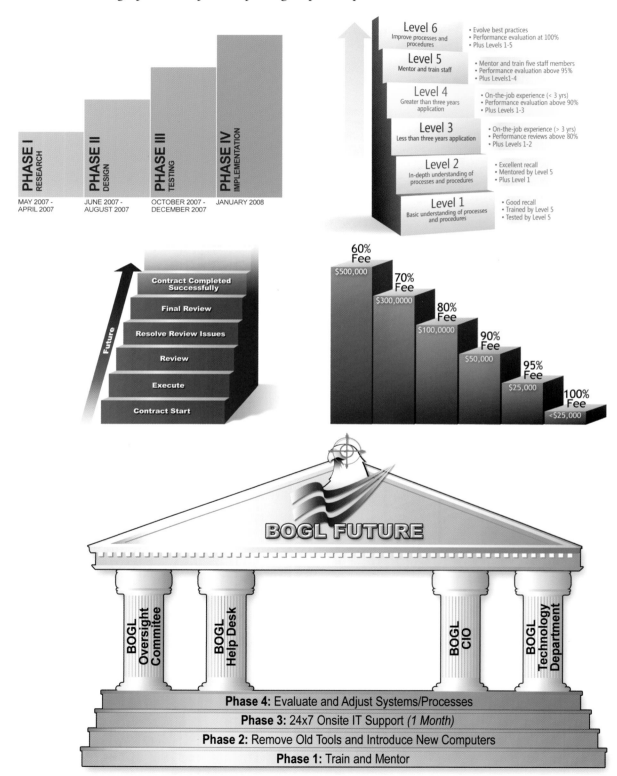

STEP-BY-STEP GRAPHIC

A graphic that depicts the execution of a linear process.

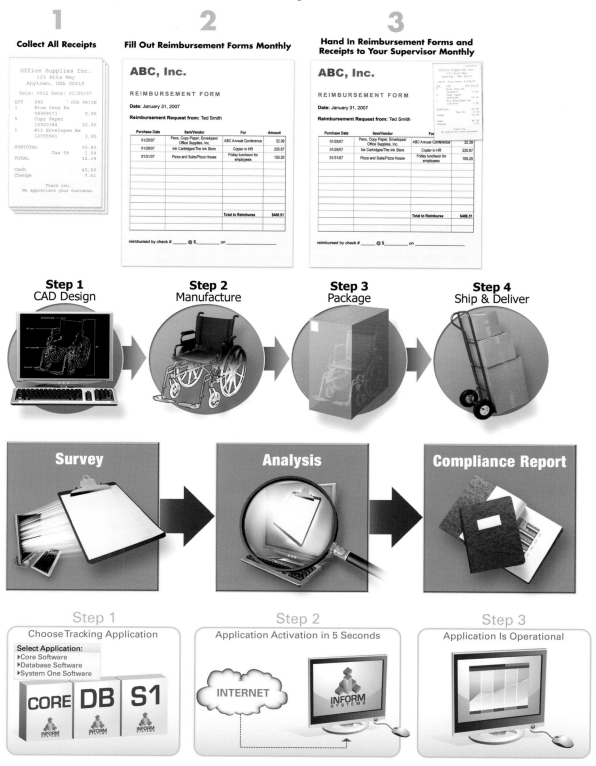

TABLE (OR MATRIX)

A grid that correlates data along multiple axes.

	Client #1	Client #2	Client #3	Client #4	Client #5	Client #6	Client #7	Client #8	Client #9	Client #10	Client #11	Client #12	Client #13	TOTAL
Number of Trainers	91	35	32	26	10	25	15	37	4	4	11	12	10	312
Number of Instructors	48	20	14	14	8	5	14	34	0	4	8	3	2	174
Number of Authors	25	7	6	10	3	0	2	4	0	4	4	3	0	68

● = In Process
✓ = Complete

	End Client	Incumbent	Sub Contractor	Task Leader	Functional Manager	Business Manager
Manage Risk Process						
• Delegate to Consultants	●	●	●	●	✓	✓
• Delegate to Temps	●	●	●	●	✓	✓
• Delegate to Janitors	●	●	●	✓	✓	✓
Manage Risks/Efforts						
• Define Effort	●	✓	✓	●		
• Define Risk			✓	●	✓	
Administer Resources						
• Resource Search (Consultants, Temps, Janitorial)	✓		●	●	✓	●
Status Reporting						
• Request Meeting			●	●	✓	●
• Assign Meeting Attendees				●		●
• Meeting Attendance	●		✓	●		✓
• Receive Credit for Project Success			✓	●		✓
• Give Credit for Project Success	✓		●	✓	✓	●

ITEM	LABOR CATEGORY	ITEM	LABOR CATEGORY
Job #1		**Job #2**	
001-A	Engineer—Beginners	002-A	Specialist—Beginner
001-B	Engineer—Advanced	002-B	Specialist—Advanced
001-C	Engineer—Senior	002-C	Specialist—Senior
Job #3		**Job #4**	
003-A	SME	004-A	Program Manager
003-B	SME Advisor	004-B	Executive Assistant

	Small Company		Mid-size Company		Large Company	
	Strategic Planning, Inc.	Digital Dimensions	Diamond Design Developers	Trinity Solutions	DELTA TECHNOLOGIES	INFORM SYSTEMS
Years in Operation	3	7	15	17	25	21
Number of Employees	8	20	63	54	345	567
Gross Profits (last year)	$500K	$1.1M	$6.2M	$7.5M	$15M	$20.5M
Projected Year End Profits	$750K	$1.5M	$6.5M	$8M	$12M	$25M
Estimated Value	$1.2M	$3M	$10.2M	$12.2M	$30M	$85.2M

Timeline

A graphic that linearly represents time.

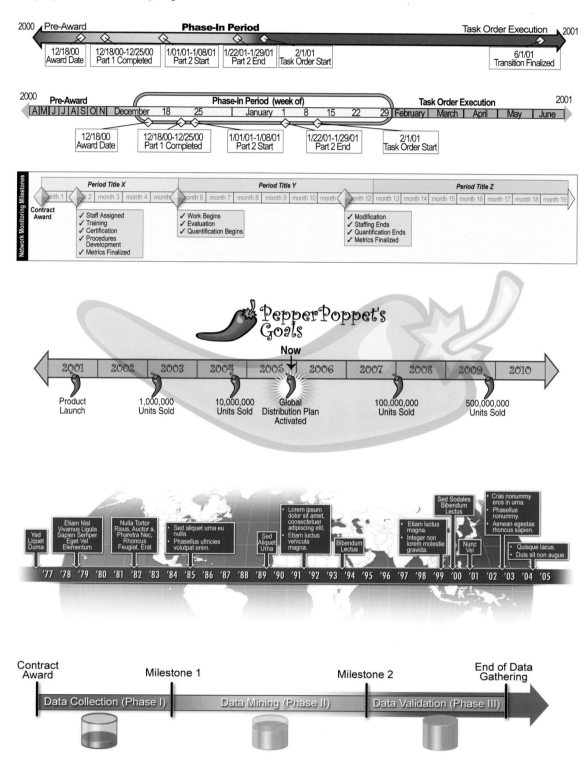

Vee Diagram

A type of process diagram that illustrates the relationships (between the two arms of the "v" shape) and verification path of interoperable elements.

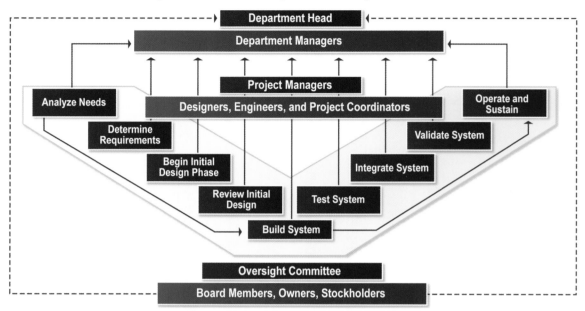

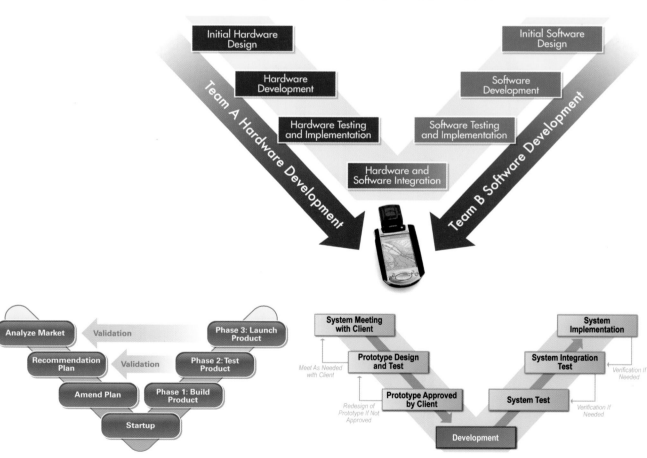

VENN DIAGRAM

A graphic that shows the relationship and/or synergy of disparate elements through the overlap of those elements.

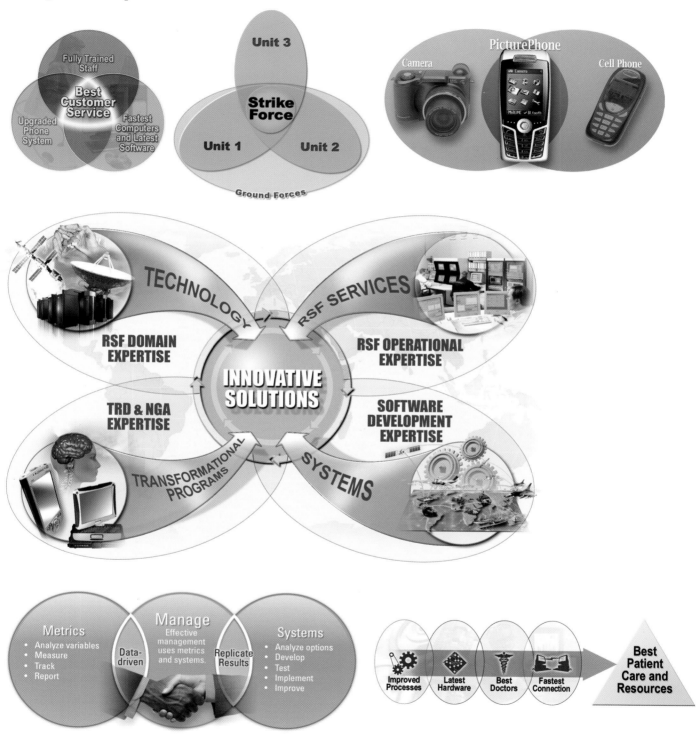

Waterfall Diagram

A type of process diagram that depicts the linear flow of steps in a progressive nature.

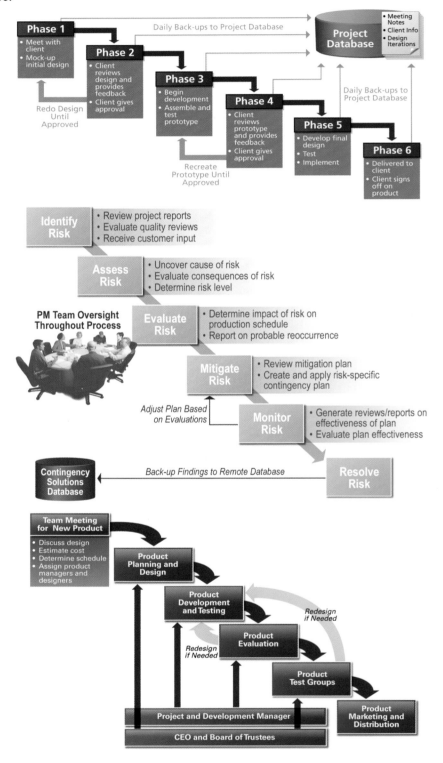

CHAPTER 7: CONCLUSION

Now you have the tools to turn any idea into a persuasive visual. Do not be intimidated by the conceptualization process. It is something you do everyday! When you give directions, tell an interesting story, research a topic, or explain your point of view, you use the same thought processes. Do you point when someone asks for directions? When you describe an action, what do your hands do? Have you ever said to a colleague "let me show you" then physically stepped through the process when words alone failed to explain? That's visual communication!

Your ability to turn words into pictures is innate. We learn to interpret what we see as babies and speak with gestures before we can talk. We are visual thinkers. For example, think "piece of pie." Did an image of a pie pop into your mind? How about "sad?" Did you see the word "sad" in your mind or a visual representation of the concept? When someone says "the house was huge," do you imagine a palatial home? It is time to tap into your talents for visual communication and use them to help you succeed. The conceptualization process presented in this book has given you that power.

After reading this book, you possess the knowledge to break down how each graphic was created and what makes it effective. Be aware of the visuals when you watch television, read magazines and newspapers, look at advertisements, and view presentations and business materials. Why do charitable organizations show images of the needy? What makes one business graphic better than another? What makes a novel stand out on the shelves at your local bookstore? Why do news programs show shocking images of an accident? Why do ads use attractive people? Start practicing by analyzing the visuals around you.

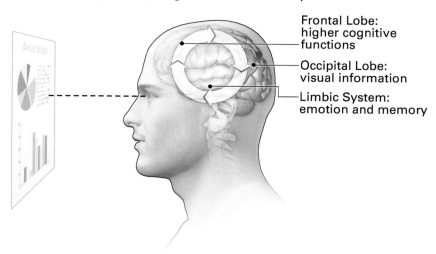

The key to conceptualizing successful graphics is to target both the cognitive and emotional functions of the brain. Your goal is to effectively communicate information while affecting your audience's state of mind.

Practice makes perfect. The more you do it, the easier it becomes. In time, the formal process will become a habit. The P.A.Q.S., four methodologies, design techniques, and strategies for generating positive feelings in your audience will become second nature as you practice conceptualizing graphics.

Creating a graphic is challenging, fun, and addictive. Once you create a successful visual, you will be hooked. Your daily communications will begin to include more and more visual explanations. You are training yourself to better use your mind's natural ability to imagine new ways of sharing ideas—to communicate with visuals. Harnessing this skill is a powerful means to achieve your goals. Through visuals, you will successfully communicate, influence, and motivate others. **Your success rate will sky rocket.**

TESTING WHAT YOU'VE LEARNED

1) Which of the four methods (Literal, Substitution, Quantitative, or Assembly) is best suited for the following:

   a) Our revenue has increased 27% this year with the greatest gain in the third quarter.

   b) We deliver an integrated IT solution. We utilize state-of-the-art technology to provide an enterprise-wide management approach. The following are included in our service-level agreement: service mapping, fault management, disaster recovery, security management, storage management, mainframe solutions, IT training, help desk support, and risk mitigation tools.

   c) The heart is divided into four chambers: Right Atrium, Right Ventricle, Left Atrium, and the Left Ventricle. Four valves connect the chambers: Pulmonary valve (at the exit of the Right Ventricle), Tricuspid (at the exit of the Right Atrium) valve, Mitral valve (at the exit of the Left atrium), and the Aortic valve (at the exit of the Left Ventricle).

   d) Today, BOGL Corporation employs 217 people. In the near future, our oversight committee will apply its 5 Point Evaluation Process to reduce the number of employees to 94.

   e) The mystery of Sudden Infant Death Syndrome (SIDS) has been solved!

   f) Routers are electronic devices designed to send enormous volumes of digital data packets speeding to their destinations along thousands of Internet pathways.

   g) Gossard Fine Homes is the premiere builder of exclusive homes in North America. Our homes continue to exceed the expectations of our most discerning clients with unimaginable beauty, flow, and functionality. Winner of fifteen awards in many areas of excellence, Gossard Fine Homes is the builder for you!

   h) The key parts of a four-stroke engine are the camshaft, crankshaft, cylinder, piston, spark plug, and valve. The cylinder's path within the piston (up or down) is known as a stroke. The downward stroke is called a power stroke because it is during this movement that the air-fuel mix in the cylinder is ignited.

2) Sketch three ways you could show interaction between the following.

3) What two design techniques could you use to add a detailed explanation to the "Create Program" box in the following process diagram?

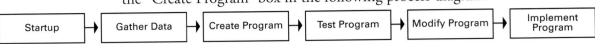

4) Sketch how you would make this graphic more ordered.

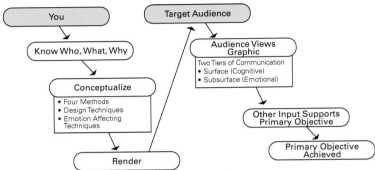

5) How would you decrease the height of this graphic without losing the smaller values?

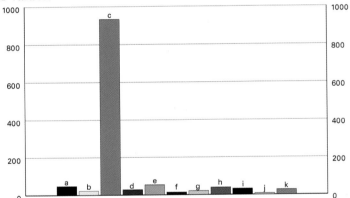

6) Using Greed, conceptualize a graphic that communicates the need for your teen audience to attend college.

7) Using the Fear of Loss, conceptualize a graphic that communicates the need for your teen audience to attend college.

8) How could you use Familiarity to conceptualize a print advertisement for your local grocery store?

9) Look through your favorite periodical and analyze the ads that use Positive Imagery to influence your decision to buy.

10) Choose your favorite advertisement in the same periodical and using Positive Imagery conceptualize an ad that would have been more effective. (Assume that you are the target audience.)

11) Using Negative Imagery, conceptualize a graphic compels your target audience to donate money to your favorite charity.

12) Why should you use horizontal and vertical lines in your visuals?

13) Why should you avoid visual noise?

14) What font is the best choice for the following graphic? Why?

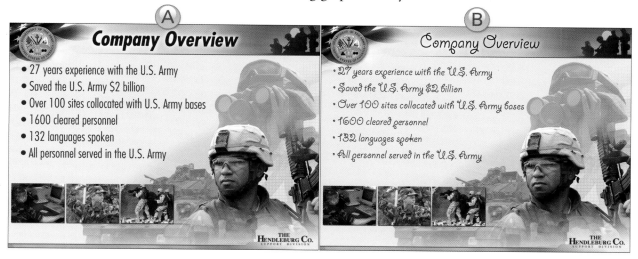

15) Consistency breeds _____ in your target audience.

16) When rendering (or directing the rendering of) a graphic teaching the U.S. Air Force how to use their new navigation system, what colors would you use? What style would you use?

17) Have you seen a PowerPoint presentation that used text too small to read? How did you feel?

18) Look through several different types of periodicals targeted to different audiences. Is there a difference in rendering style? How did each style make you feel?

19) Which graphic style is appropriate for empirical analysis?

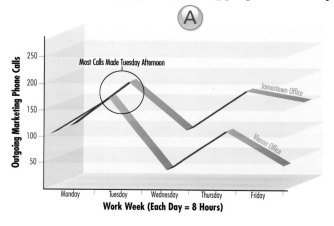

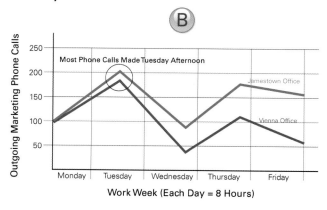

20) What are the three traps that cause most graphics to fail?

21) What are the seven strategies to avoid the three traps?

22) Can you think of a time when you were presented with a graphic that was confusing? Why was it confusing?

23) Which rule does this graphic break?

24) Why is it more important to get it right rather than be innovative?

25) Which rule does this graphic break?

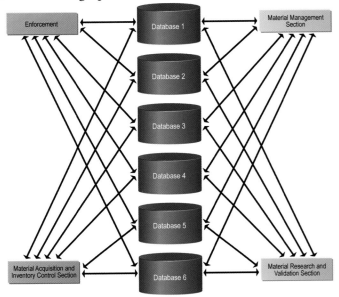

26) Why should you make your graphic audience focused?

27) When should you use the least amount of aesthetic embellishment?

28) What is "razzle dazzle"?

(See page 139 for the answers.)

ANSWERS

1) (a) Quantitative, (b) Assembly, (c) Literal and/or Assembly,
(d) Quantitative, (e) Substitution or Literal, (f) Substitution or Literal,
(g) Literal, (h) Literal and/or Assembly if the text was too confusing

2)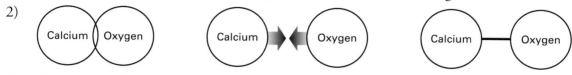

3) Blowout or callout

4)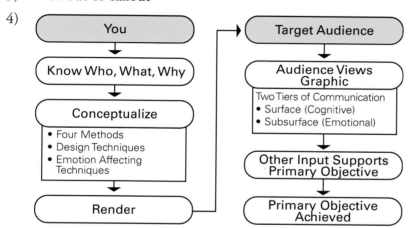

5) Use a scalebreak

6) Perhaps you focused on the financial security gained from higher education?

7) Perhaps you focused on the money lost as a result of not receiving a higher education?

8) Perhaps you showed the store or a well-liked person?

9) Consider what stood out most and why.

10) Consider what was most appealing about the ad.

11) See page 59.

12) Horizontal and vertical shapes and lines provide a sense of stability. Using a horizontal and vertical layout communicates that the presented information is organized and controlled.

13) Because too much visual noise results in a hard-to-follow, difficult-to-read graphic. The net effect is usually a negative opinion of the subject matter or presenter.

14) Ⓐ is more appropriate for the target audience and subject matter (less whimsical than the font in Ⓑ) and it is more legible.

15) Trust

16) Air Force blue and patriotic colors (red, white, and blue). Avoid the use of canned clip art and use images of Air Force personnel and equipment.

17) Annoyed? Disinterested? Lost?

18) Consider how the styles and visual elements are related to the periodical's target audience.

19) Ⓑ

20) Over complication, under clarification, and poor rendering

21) The seven strategies to avoid the three traps are
   - All aesthetic decisions should have a purpose
   - Stay consistent
   - Getting graphics right is far more important than being innovative
   - Keep graphics clean and simple
   - Label elements
   - Use recognizable imagery
   - Focus on your audience

22) Consider how it made you feel and affected your perception of the presenter/company.

23) Label elements.

24) Being innovative at the cost of clarity often results in failure.

25) Keep graphics clean and simple.

26) Because it is all about your audience. They are the reason you are creating your visual. Ignoring them results in the failure to achieve your graphic's primary objective.

27) When presenting a graphic that has the singular objective to convey data and nothing more, use no aesthetic embellishment.

28) "Razzle dazzle"—the author or designer, purposefully or not, uses attractive or dense visuals or a complicated layout rather than focusing on the audience's needs.

GLOSSARY

Aesthetics – A set of principles regarding the nature and appreciation of beauty. The study of aesthetics increased the validity of many critical judgments concerning art. The established aesthetic principles create a shared vocabulary and understanding for the objective evaluation of beauty.

Analogy (visual) – A graphic depiction of an action, concept, or entity that augments (having a logical relevance to that which is augmented) another action, concept, or entity making a comparison in an effort to improve communication. A visual analogy compares a variety of attributes. It is often used to form logical arguments: if two different things are similar in one way, they might be similar in other ways as well.

Area Chart – A graphic that depicts continuous quantitative data usually over time and uses filled areas to communicate amounts, time frames, or values.

Assembly Method – A process for conceptualizing graphics by capturing important chunks of information and assembling them (like building blocks) in a way that better communicates their relationships or interactions.

Author – The graphic's content creator. The person(s) who is the source of the information contained in the graphic. Often the author directs the creation of the graphic.

Balance (visual) – Balance is achieved when the visual "weight" of both halves of a graphic is similar giving a sense of equilibrium.

Bar Chart – A graphic that depicts the changes in quantitative data using "bars," where the size of each bar represents the proportional value of the quantitative data.

Before and After Graphic – A graphic that compares the "as is" or "before" state to the "to be" or "after" state.

Bridge Graphic – A graphic metaphor depicting the connection or transition between two actions, concepts, or entities.

Bubble Chart – A graphic that uses circles or spheres to show ranges of quantitative data. It can also illustrate the uncertainty of predicted value.

Building Blocks – A graphic that interconnects data to illustrate how elements work together to create a larger unit.

Calendar – A table showing years (or a year), months, weeks, and days.

Candlestick Chart – A chart traditionally used to analyze values and sales of stocks, bonds, commodities, etc. Price is shown in the vertical axis and time in the horizontal axis.

Chunking – Breaking content into bite-sized chunks that can then be reassembled to show an overview of the content presented.

Circle Charts – A family of graphics that display quantitative data using a circular format and includes radar graphs, sector graphs, circle column graphs, and many similarly shaped graphics.

Collage – A graphic that is composed of juxtaposed images.

Conceptualization – The process of creating a design or design plan. Effective conceptualization requires research and visualization.

Conveyor Belt Graphic – A graphic metaphor that depicts a repeatable linear process.

Cross Section Diagram – A graphic where an entity or depiction of a concept is cut in half so the different layers that make up the whole can be viewed and individually defined.

Cutaway Diagram – This graphic is similar to a cross section diagram where you can see the inner workings or mechanics of an entity or depiction of a concept viewed through a missing or transparent portion of the outermost layer.

Dashboard Graphic – A graphic that presents multiple metrics (potentially using multiple graphic types) in one consolidated format. (Think of a car's dashboard.)

Design Techniques – Ways of illustrating concepts.

Discriminator – A function, feature, or characteristic that differentiates one product, service, or idea from another.

Dome Graphic – A graphic that looks like a "snow globe" illustrating the containment of elements. (The dome graphic is especially good at communicating protection/security.)

Earned Value Management System (EVMS) Chart – A risk probability schedule graphic. Used to show how potential changes in a budget at different milestones can have a ripple effect on costs later in the process.

Exploded Diagram – A graphic showing the disassembled parts of an entity or concept placed in a manner that indicates their relative positions when reassembled.

Floor Plan – A graphic depicting the layout of a room(s) or level(s) in a building.

Flow Chart – See Process Diagram.

Funnel Graphic – A graphic metaphor showing the passing of elements through a conduit (the funnel) resulting in the effective allocation, consolidation, and/or organization of those elements.

Gantt Chart – A bar chart representing time and activity used for planning, tracking, and controlling schedules.

Gauge Graphic – A graphic metaphor using readouts and measurement tools to depict data for analysis.

Gear Graphic – A graphic metaphor depicting how parts work together and often illustrates processes and interoperability.

Highlighting – Using contrasting colors, shades, sizes, and visual complexity to draw attention to an element in a graphic.

Icon – A representational graphic element that is visually analogous with an action, concept, or entity.

Illustration – A visual representation that is used to make the subject more appealing or easier to understand.

Information Graphic – Any graphic that clarifies and/or explains.

Line Chart – A graphic showing the changes in quantitative data using lines, where the position of a line represents the proportional value of the data.

Literal Method – A process for conceptualizing graphics by showing exactly what is described or stated as a way to clarify, explain, or support a claim.

Looping Graphic – A graphic that depicts a repeating process or event.

Map Graphic – A graphic showing a region of physical space: a continent, country, city, office building, etc.

Matrix – See Table.

Metaphor (visual) – A graphic depiction of an action, concept, or entity that replaces (having the same applicable characteristics as that which is replaced) another action, concept, or entity making an implicit comparison in an effort to improve communication. Essentially, replace one entity or concept for another where the replacement shares the same applicable characteristics.

Method – An approach for conceptualizing successful graphics.

Mindshare – The awareness of a company, product, service, or idea.

Network Diagram – A diagram showing the connections between elements that compose a network.

Noise (visual) – Many visual elements or "busy" textures/imagery.

Ockham's Razor – A widely accepted and proven postulate asserting that simplicity in design is preferred over complexity.

Organizational Chart – A graphic depicting the hierarchy, arrangement, structure, and/or relationship of a group of elements. (Typically, an organization and its personnel are the subject matter.)

Path Graphic – See Road Graphic.

Peg Graphic – A graphic showing the interconnectivity of entities or ideas to create a unified whole (think Legos®).

Photograph – A picture of a person, place, or thing.

Pie Chart (also called a Segmented Chart) – A graphic that communicates percentages of the whole using proportional segments.

Pipe Graphic – A graphic metaphor representing the isolated linear flow of elements.

Point Chart – A graphic that shows quantitative data using plotted points.

Presenter – The person, place, or thing most associated with the graphic in the mind of the audience.

- A mall map kiosk: The mall is the presenter.
- A PowerPoint presentation: Either the orator(s) or the entity (i.e., company or association) for whom the presentation was created is the presenter.
- Vehicle maintenance instructions: The vehicle manufacturer or dealership is the presenter.

Primary Objective – The main goal of a graphic.

Process Diagram (also called a Flow Chart) – A graphic showing the flow or progression of steps in a process or event.

Puzzle Graphic – A graphic metaphor representing the synergy of separate elements that creates a new whole.

Pyramid Graphic – A graphic metaphor that depicts hierarchy, arrangement, structure, and/or relationship of a group of elements. The bottom elements support the elements above.

Quantitative Method – A process for conceptualizing graphics by capturing descriptions of quantity (value, amount, or time) and choosing one of thirteen quantitative graphic types to communicate that data.

Render – The physical creation (in any media) of the graphic.

Risk Matrix – A table that depicts varying levels of risk as affected by the influences of one or more variables.

Road Graphic – A graphic metaphor depicting the path between the "as is" or "before" state to the "to be" or "after" state.

Scale Graphic – A graphic metaphor that illustrates comparison.

Segmented Chart – See Pie Chart.

Simile (visual) – A graphic depiction of an action, concept, or entity that augments (having a logical relevance to that which is augmented) another action, concept, or entity making a comparison in an effort to improve communication.

Spiral Graphic – A graphic metaphor that illustrates the evolution of an action, concept, or entity through a cyclical process.

Stacked Diagram – A graphic that depicts the hierarchy, arrangement, structure, and/or relationship of a group of elements. A stacked diagram can also show flow or a progression of steps in a process similar to a pyramid and/or process diagram but can be more versatile.

Stair Graphic – A graphic metaphor depicting steps in a process.

Step-by-Step Graphic – A graphic that depicts the execution of a linear process.

Substitution Method – A process for conceptualizing graphics by substituting one action, concept, or entity for another—using a visual metaphor, analogy, or simile—to better clarify or explain information.

Subsurface (Emotional) Communication – Subconscious effects a graphic and its content have on our emotional state, our state of mind.

Surface (Cognitive) Communication – Conscious comprehension of the data presented in the graphic.

Symbol – A representational graphic element that has a learned meaning or accepted connotation for an action, concept, or entity.

System/Enterprise Architecture – A graphic showing the architecture of a system or enterprise.

Symmetry (visual) – Equally divide a graphic in half using a central axis as the dividing line (usually vertically or horizontally divided). The more alike both halves are, the more symmetrical the image.

Table (also called a Matrix) – A grid that correlates data along two axes. A lengthier but more descriptive definition is an array of rows and columns (arranged in a grid) interconnecting elements. The point of row and column convergence reveals the data that links the action, concept, or entity indicated in the row title and the column title.

Target Audience – The person(s) for whom the graphic was intended.

10 Second Rule – A widely accepted and proven postulate that the target audience needs to know and understand the main point (the most important message) of a graphic within 10 seconds or else the graphic will fail to achieve its primary objective.

Timeline – A graphic that linearly represents time.

Vee Diagram – A type of process diagram that illustrates the relationships (between the two arms of the "v" shape) and verification path of interoperable elements.

Venn Diagram – A graphic that shows the relationship and/or synergy of disparate elements through the overlap of those elements.

Visual Noise – Too many visual elements or "busy" textures/imagery in a graphic. Visual noise often induces a negative opinion of the subject matter.

Visualization – To see the graphic components in your mind's eye before rendering.

Waterfall Diagram – A type of process diagram that depicts the linear flow of steps in a progressive nature.

INDEX

TOOLS THAT HELP YOU SUCCEED...

BUSINESS GRAPHICS ON DVD

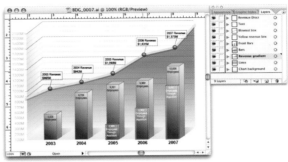

The BDG Master Collection Source Art DVD contains 111 **editable** graphics plus 41 **bonus** graphics (and a free copy of the original *Billion Dollar Graphics* eBook set and more). All graphics are professionally conceptualized and rendered at print resolution and editable in Adobe Illustrator and Photoshop CS2 or newer for both Mac and Windows. These powerful visuals are made specifically to help you communicate your messages quickly and clearly and increase your success rate. The time and cost savings will pay for your new library of source art the first time you use it. The BDG Master Collection is a **wise investment** for any professional. Get your low-cost business graphics on DVD before they are gone at www.BillionDollarGraphics.com.

POWERPOINT TEMPLATES ON DVD

Make an impression with new, high-end, unique Microsoft PowerPoint templates. Tailor your template to your audience

Title Slide

Single Stacked Title Bar

Double Stacked Title Bar

and subject matter and have a positive impact at your next presentation. You get 125 high-quality, professional PowerPoint template sets plus **hundreds** of color variations. These 125 PowerPoint template sets comprise three print resolution template slides: title slide, single stacked title bar slide, and double stacked title bar slide (for longer titles). Get your new professional PowerPoint template DVD now at www.BillionDollarGraphics.com.

Graphics Training

Stop losing time and money doing graphics the wrong way. Learn to transform anything into clear, compelling graphics that grow your business and lower cost. **NO design skill required.** Turn your old graphics, words, and ideas into powerful graphics for *immediate* use during the course.

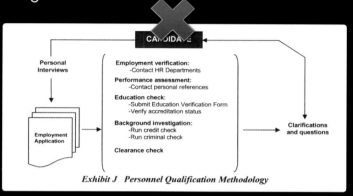

> "The power in the process is that it **eliminates rewrites**, gets the message right, and validates your approach all at the same time. It really **validates the whole proposal solution**."
> —Bob Gillette, CRI

If you need your next presentation, proposal, sales or marketing effort, training event, or technical document to be successful, then you need clear, communicative, compelling graphics. You have very little time to convince your audience that you and your content are the best-of-the-best. Graphics communicate volumes about you, your company, and your product or service **in seconds**. You say your company and solution are the best, then your business materials need to support that assertion.

Companies like HP, Motorola, Raytheon, Lockheed Martin, Staubach Company, and Northrop Grumman lowered their cost and increased their success rates with Billion Dollar Graphics training. (You **need** a proven, repeatable process to stay competitive in today's market.)

Contact us now at info@BillionDollarGraphics.com and mention this book to **get 20% off** on any training package.

> "Mike showed us that if you use the right tools and methodology, getting technical abstract thought on paper and transforming it into a visual that [your audience] understands does not have to be an overwhelming dilemma. Mike's training session was **an immediate hit**.
> —Kathy Furlong, Nortel

> "In the end … we had real and practical knowledge for developing graphics **quickly and easily**. We've had **very positive reactions**…"
> —Randy Thomas, Wellpoint

Transform

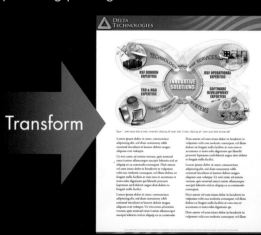

Email info@BillionDollarGraphics.com now and save 20%

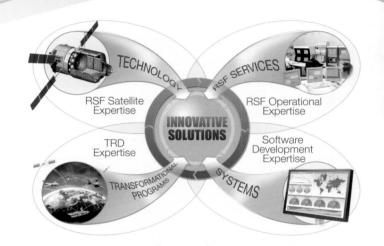

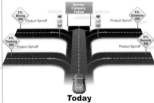
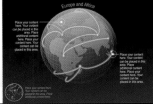

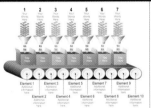
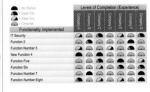

Your Bonus Virtual CD

Step 1: Go to www.BillionDollarGraphics.com/VCD.

Step 2: Follow the simple instructions.

Step 3: Get your *bonus* graphics, tools, secrets, tips, tricks, and best practices.

The Virtual CD content will be updated over time. Be sure to visit often to see what's new!